DONATED BY:

JEFFREY CAMINSKY

*A book is a garden
carried in the pocket.*

The Sonnets of William Shakespeare

The Sonnets of William Shakespeare

Edited, with notes and commentary
by Jeffrey Caminsky

NEW ALEXANDRIA PRESS
LIVONIA

Published by New Alexandria Press
PO Box 530516
Livonia, Michigan 48153
www.newalexandriapress.com

The poems contained in this edition were originally published in London in 1609 as *Shake-speare's sonnets*. The intervening centuries have seen countless editions, annotations, and commentaries in print.

Illustrations and cover design by Jeffrey Caminsky. The cover image is adapted from a rendition of the statue in Leicester Square in London, England. The image of the author appearing at the end of the book is adapted from a rendition of Shakespeare's portrait appearing on his First Folio.

Hardcover Edition:
ISBN-10: 0-9790106-5-9
ISBN-13: 978-0-9790106-5-1

Softcover Edition:
ISBN-10: 0-9790106-2-4
ISBN-13: 978-0-9790106-2-0

Quantity discounts are available on bulk purchases of this book Special books or book excerpts can also be made available to fit specific needs. For information, please contact *sales@newalexandriapress.com* or send written inquiries to New Alexandria Press, PO Box 530516, Livonia, Michigan 48153.

Printed in the United States of America
First Printing October 2008

10 9 8 7 6 5 4 3 2 1
First Edition

2008934582

To my father, the poet....

Contents

Editor's Note

THIS VOLUME WILL PROBABLY OFFER little help to the advanced scholar. The works cited in the bibliography are generally well known, and the insights offered in the following pages may seem commonplace and prosaic to those who have made the study of William Shakespeare their life's work. Instead, it is hoped that this work will assist those beginning their study of one of the world's greatest writers by showing that Shakespeare is not the sterile literary monument of the typical English literature class, but rather the witty, often bawdy humanist who captivated audiences in his own day and has spoken to every generation since.

These days, many approach Shakespeare with dread. A glance at the formal structure of his plays and poems, the many quaint and unfamiliar words, and the pretty though lofty-sounding passages, can tempt the reader to recoil in apprehension, convinced that whatever greatness lurks inside is beyond the comprehension of any but the stuffy and bespectacled. In fact, however, what Shakespeare wrote resonated with the common people of his day—who were, on the whole, no better educated than we are, despite their ability to understand the Bard of Avon without resorting to notes or commentary. His words, even if unfamiliar to us today, were never crafted to confuse. Rather, he sought to entertain; to make us think; and to provoke us to tears or laughter, often at the same time.

The sonnets, while hardly his most ambitious or meaty works, are in many ways his most accessible. They are short, as sonnets always are; they are largely self-contained; and their recurring subject is one familiar to every human who has ever walked on this planet: love, and all the joys, frustrations, and pratfalls that accompany human affection in all its forms.

The interpretive notes that accompany each of the sonnets are meant to provide some guidance to the reader unfamiliar with the vocabulary or formal conventions of Elizabethan poetry. Despite what the reader may come to think, they are intended to be helpful—and the short synopsis that opens each note is not meant to insult the reader's intelligence, but to provide a quick context for the poem. Even so, they will probably not answer every question the reader will have and may, at times, merely state the obvious. In addition, the complex and intricate nuances contained throughout Shakespeare's work relied upon the language of the day—a language which is still growing and changing, and will do so as long as English-speakers use their tongues to describe our changing world in inventive ways. Where appropriate, the notes try to convey some small hint of various shadings of meaning suggested by the language, to give the reader a sense of the wordplay that made Shakespeare such an engaging and creative writer. Unfortunately, this particular writer is more than a match for any editor—and the reader is likely to discover that, as with any great artist, there is no end to the discoveries that unfold with each new level of comprehension that waits to be found in the playful writings of the greatest writer the world has yet seen.

It is the editor's hope that the reader will come away having gained not only a richer understanding of some of the most sensitive love poems ever to flow from a poet's pen, but also with fewer apprehensions about delving into the substance of Shake-speare's more challenging works.

JC
September, 2008

The Sonnets of William Shakespeare

Introduction

SHAKESPEARE'S ENGLAND OFTEN seems far removed from our modern, 21st Century lives. Coming a few hundred years after the Crusades, in the depths of the Little Ice Age that saw glaciers advancing and bitter cold gripping the planet, it was nevertheless a time of endless possibilities. The New World* had just been opened to settlement, ships were sailing around the world, the end of the Dark Ages had ushered in an age of reason and enlightenment,** and European writers and thinkers were stretching the arts and sciences to new heights. In Italy, these were the days of Galileo; in Spain, Cervantes was laying the foundation for modern Spanish literature—even as the Inquisition was rising to crush the spirit of religious unorthodoxy; and Elizabethan England, having defeated the Spanish Armada, was enjoying its own cultural blossoming, with William Shakespeare and a host of poets and thinkers laying much of the artistic and scientific framework for Western thought in the years to come.

And yet at the human level the people of Shakespeare's day were no different from us—or, indeed, from humans of any generation since the dawn of time. Love and joy, loss and redemption, vengeance and mercy, hatred and despair, are emotions human beings have experienced throughout our time on this planet. Life, for all its twists and turns, remains much as it always has: a search for happiness, while looking for enough food, and plenty of sex.***

---

*Well, new to the Europeans.

**Compared, that is, to the Middle Ages. In other respects, humanity was showing as little rationality as ever.

***Elizabethans were, after all, a lusty lot. This facet of olden times is often overlooked in literature classes but, as shown below, soon becomes apparent to any careful reader of Shakespeare.

The Sonnets of William Shakespeare

Despite the arcane scholarship dealing with the greatest writer the English language has produced, Shakespeare did not write to impress professors of literature, and it is doubtful that he wielded his timeless grace and artistry just to show how talented he was. It is likely that he wrote for the reason writers have always written: he had things he wanted to say, and something in his soul made him want to share his ideas with the world. He infused his writing with beauty because he could find beauty in everything. But he was well acquainted with the baser side of human nature as well—the lust for power and thirst for revenge—that sets the stage for the human drama, the eternal struggle between good and evil.

If we view Shakespeare not as a relic, but as a living human being, we see at once both his playfulness and his passion. His wit was unsurpassed, and we might well suppose that his capacity for enjoying life was the equal of anyone we might meet today. And so if we view his writing as an expression of his moods and emotions, rather than some tablet writ by the gods, we can see in his poetry all the elements of fun and sorrow we experience in our own lives. His teasing of friends and lovers is no less playful merely because it comes from Shakespeare. And if we try to sense the human being behind the marble mask we study in our literature classes, we will see a dimension and spark to his writing that makes it come suddenly to life.

The ancient Greeks wrote of gods and immortal heroes, but their plays and poems reflected the reality that they saw around them. Today, advances in science and technology may let our modern imaginations wander among the stars, but the realities we invent for our amusement will always reflect our own world. So, too, Shakespeare wrote of the universe that he lived in—an age of discovery, filled with history and legends, passions and turmoil, royalty and knaves. And yet like all great writers, his stories and poems speak to something deeper in the human condition. The music of his language sounds quaint and almost foreign to modern ears; but if we look beyond the courtliness of Elizabethan expression to embrace the spirit and sentiments the writer is conveying, we can almost touch the soul that gave voice to some of the loveliest, most profound thoughts that ever flowed from a writer's pen.

Much modern scholarship deprives Shakespeare of his heart: so much attention is devoted to his artistry and influence on the development of modern English that we often miss the elegant simplicity of his wisdom, and the knowing and witty soul that loved to poke fun at life, and everyone around him. Far from the sterile legend of the typical English literature class he is instead playful; he is bawdy; he is profound; and while he obviously took great care about his writing, he never took himself as seriously as modern scholars do. That is, perhaps, the key to enjoying Shakespeare: recognizing that his art was meant to be experienced and savored, rather than labored over and studied to death.

Who was Shakespeare?

In his day, William Shakespeare was a well-known actor and theater owner, of no particular outward sophistication that we can discern across the abyss of time. And yet Shakespeare the Writer exhibited an exquisite use of language, wit, and a highly sophisticated sense of court etiquette, history, and the political nuances of the day, making it obvious that the writer was not only a keenly observant student of human behavior, but also a highly cultured man of some prominence. This has led some to conclude that he would doubtless have wished to remain anonymous, to avoid the scandal that would have resulted from association with theater types and other ruffians. And in turn, this all convinces some that Shakespeare the Theater Owner was merely the public face for a brilliant humanist and visionary whose innovative work reinvented theater as an art form and resonates in the human soul to this day. Others identified as the "real" Shakespeare include Christopher Marlowe, Sir Francis Bacon, Edward de Vere, the Earl of Oxford—and Queen Elizabeth herself. The writer could not, in this view, be someone without a proper university education, leading doubters on a quest to uncover the hidden signs and clues needed to unravel the mysteries.

Often forgotten amid these lofty debates is the practical fact that in the tumultuous days of Tudor England, a young Stratford boy with a Roman Catholic mother, whose father had suffered a financial downturn just at the time that the boy might have entertained dreams of heading off to university, would have faced formidable hurdles completing his formal education. In addition, the struggles of a talented writer in any era are daunting enough. When we add in the cultural struggles of the Reformation, we see that Shakespeare's personal and professional difficulties probably left him little time for pursuing academic or professional credentials. He was, in all likelihood, busy enough writing.

For various reasons—among them the fact that the plays and poems attributed to William Shakespeare appear to coincide with specific events in his own life, and end shortly before his death in 1616—there are problems with every alternative except the simplest (and, if we trust to Ockham's Razor, the likeliest): the writings attributed to William Shakespeare in his day were actually written by William Shakespeare.* In addition, the public acclaim he received during his lifetime—by the age of thirty he was one of the best-known and most admired writers of his generation—makes it unlikely that there was a secret writer behind the public mask.

Much speculation about the "authenticity" of Shakespeare's authorship stems from a disbelief that a common, ordinary actor and theater manager was capable of producing some of the most enduring poetic literature of all time. In his own day, this snobbishness appeared in its own way: one famous poet and playwright of the time—Robert Greene, an educated and sophisticated writer who was also among the first successful novelists—was so distressed by the success of "an upstart Crow" that shortly before his own death in 1592 he penned a swan-song piece denouncing Shakespeare's

---

*Among the many problems with the skeptics' arguments is the fact that the "Will" sonnets—*ie*, Sonnets 135-136—as well as various puns on "will" scattered throughout the poems, make little sense if the poet writing them was really named Christopher, Francis, or Edward.

Introduction

temerity as a mere actor to presume to "bombast out a blanke verse" as a writer.* While known by this time as an actor and poet of growing repute, it appears that Shakespeare's first play—opening the saga of *Henry the Sixth* and the War of the Roses, and inventing historical drama for the English stage—had opened earlier in the year, immediately enjoying widespread praise and acclaim. That other men of letters may have felt a measure of professional jealousy from the start of Shakespeare's career as a playwright, and the disdain Greene and others may have shown toward the limits of his formal education, seems to confirm not only that his unique gifts as a writer were recognized at once, but also that the author's identity was not seriously in dispute among his contemporaries.** Moreover, much of the richness of Shakespeare's plays comes from the vivid sense of realism resulting from his depiction of real people—common folk as well as royalty—and hints and traces of his rural upbringing that appear throughout his work.***

---

* *Greene's Groatsworth of Wit*, published posthumously, appears to have been the repository for various resentments collected throughout the writer's life. He did, however, aim most of his vitriol at the "upstart Crow," who had the gall to display talent beyond his station—and Greene may well have had help, for other members of the educated class of writers at the time had their own snobbish tendencies to sustain them. But the publisher hastily disclaimed any responsibility for the content of the pamphlet—a sign, perhaps, that the Crow had patrons who did not take kindly to such ridicule.

Greene's death in poverty came largely as a result of illness brought about by excesses of his life-style. (Apparently, the excesses of the famous are not a development of modern living).

**Contemporary mentions of Shakespeare as the author of the then-published poems *Venus and Adonis*, and *Lucrece*, suggest that in addition to his plays, he made an immediate impression on the reading public as well. See, Kay, *Shakespeare: His Life, Work, and Era* (1992) pp153-162 for an account of public reaction.

***This theme is fleshed out in Stephen Greenblatt's fascinating and highly readable book on the human influences that likely shaped Shakespeare's growth into the monumental artist that still captivates the world's imagination. See Greenblatt, *Will in the World: How Shakespeare Became Shakespeare* (2004).

Genius often appears where we least expect it, so long as its seeds find fertile ground in which to grow. In Shakespeare's case, his family appears to have been reasonably prosperous and well-educated for his day: his father was among the leading citizens of the town of Stratford, and Elizabethans were hardly ignorant of the value of education. Most men of prominence in the era were literate and, as in our own day, many were sophisticated and highly cultured. Curiosity and the thirst for knowledge are hardly products of recent origin, and people have thought and wondered about the human condition for as long as mankind has existed. It is perhaps our own cultural conceit that seeks some towering figure who should rightfully adorn the bust on Stratford's monument to England's greatest writer, and looks for someone other than the plump, balding, ordinary-looking fellow whose face adorns it today. But writing is often a solitary endeavor, needing peace and quiet to produce anything of value. As a result, poets are rarely adventurers, and the lives of writers are often less interesting than the subjects they wrote about. Those disappointed in the pedestrian appearance of England's greatest writer might take solace in the transcendent grandeur of his art, and his mastery over our common tongue.

In the end, it really matters very little, except for reasons of historical curiosity: the writer we know as Shakespeare still echoes in the hearts of men and women four hundred years later. His body of work is unsurpassed in any language, and gives us insights into the human soul that can be touching, and often alarming, but which are always profound.

In a larger sense, the very fact that Shakespeare was outwardly so ordinary says something as profound about the human condition as anything he could have written. That a common man, with an uncommon mind and a timeless ability to sift through the human condition, could articulate our hopes, fears, and aspirations with such power and sensitivity is, in the end, a more liberating discovery than we would find by discovering that the writer was really a well-educated and sophisticated aristocrat like the Earl of Oxford or Sir Francis Bacon. And in many ways the idea that Shakespeare authored his own plays is really no more remarkable than the notion that a largely uneducated and self-taught man could have written the Gettysburg address. But given the sparse records about Shakespeare, it is not surprising that academic disputes about a country bumpkin from Stratford sound more plausible than those one might raise about Lincoln. For some, the mere likelihood that Shakespeare, like Lincoln, may have had a curious mind, a thirst for knowledge, and was a voracious reader with wide-ranging interests appears too subjective to settle the matter. And so the dispute over the identify of the "real" Shakespeare is likely to continue, if only to allow academics and students of English literature the same chance to pursue conspiracy theories as everyone else.[*]

Shakespeare's World

From our 21st Century vantage, the past often looks fixed and distant. Our history books contain records of wars and conflicts, and the progress of mankind from the dawn of civilization often seems dry and irrelevant to modern sensibilities attuned more to the current fads and crises of the day than to the troubles of our ancestors. But every era has its challenges to face, and its insurmountable problems to confront. Elizabethan England was no exception—and, to those wishing a richer understanding of literature, placing the writer's life in the context of its time can provide insights into his work that are both rewarding and unexpected.

---

[*]Among the more recent books claiming to solve the riddle of Shakespeare's "true" identity are Anderson, *"Shakespeare" by Another Name: A Biography of Edward de Vere, Earl of Oxford, the Man Who Was Shakespeare,* New York: Gotham, 2005; Asquith, *Shadowplay: The Hidden Beliefs and Coded Politics of William Shakespeare,* New York: Public Affairs, 2005; Fields, *Players: The Mysterious Identity of William Shakespeare,* New York: HarperCollins, 2005; Ogburn, *The Mysterious William Shakespeare: The Myth and the Reality,* New York: Dodd, Mead & Co, 1984; and Whittemore, *The Monument: Shake-speare's Sonnets by Edward de Vere, 17th Earl of Oxford,* Marshfield Hills, MA: Meadow Geese Press, 2005.

Records in Stratford place Shakespeare's birth in April of 1564, in a year when an outbreak of the plague sweeping across the countryside visited his hometown, and life expectancy in England was less than thirty years. This was also a time of religious and civil turmoil. The Protestant Reformation was in full swing, and Queen Elizabeth had recently assumed the throne after the death of Henry VIII in 1547. Her ascension to the throne began a tumultuous decade that ended with the death of Elizabeth's half-sister, the Catholic Queen Mary, known to the history books as "Bloody Mary."

At the time of William's birth, Shakespeare's father, recently arrived in town, had just been chosen alderman, and the family appears to have enjoyed some measure of prominence. John Shakespeare, already a prosperous merchant, was chosen Bailiff of Stratford (the rough equivalent of mayor) in 1568, and served in that capacity for some years.* Mary, John's wife and William's mother, came from a Catholic family, which ensured that the Shakespeares would have first-hand experience with the religious turmoil of the day. Their bright and observant eldest son would have enjoyed all the advantages of a respected and upwardly mobile family in small-town England of the Sixteenth Century—including an education at the local school—and would have found himself employed in the family glove-making business. Local festivals and visiting theater troupes, playing in the towns and villages nearby, probably sparked young Will's imagination. By the 1570s, however, a change in family fortunes was leading to his father's declining

---

*On the other hand, Shakespeare's uncle Henry—John's brother—appears to have been something of a ne'er-do-well. Where John's impression on the public records of the day stemmed largely from business or civic affairs, Uncle Henry appears to have been known for avoiding participation in road maintenance, spending time in jail for brawling or debt, and appearing in church wearing a hat, rather than a cap—thereby deliberately (or absent-mindedly; though mulish, he was also something of a slacker) violating the "Statute of Caps," an Elizabethan foray into government planning designed to shore up the sagging cap-making market.

Introduction

status and role in civic affairs,* and sometime in the 1580s, the gifted young man departed for London—leaving a wife and children behind in Stratford—to seek his fame and fortune in the big city.

William Shakespeare had married in 1582 at age of 18, to an older woman named Anne Hathaway, eight years his senior. His daughter was born six months later, and three years afterwards he and his wife had twins—one of whom died in childhood. While we may never know the circumstances that caused him to leave Stratford, within a short time after his move to London he had become a well-known actor with a playing company that would come to be known as the Lord Chamberlain's Men, and a poet of growing renown. In 1592, four years after the defeat of the Spanish Armada by the British Navy and a provident storm in the English Channel, we find records of a play attributed to him performed in London: the First Part of *Henry the Sixth*, performed on March 3rd, found immediate acclaim and a high level of commercial success, propelling the author's career to new levels and introducing a towering figure to the world of literature.**

---

*Beginning in the late 1570s, John Shakespeare began liquidating most of his property and holdings—something that suggests a major financial crisis in his life. The source of this decline is a matter of considerable speculation: it could have simply reflected a serious decline in the local economy, although the business acumen displayed by John and William throughout their lives suggests that they would have been able to weather most cyclical downturns. Another possibility is a crackdown in "wool brogging"—the trafficking in wool by persons not licensed to trade in that lucrative commodity, which had been a considerable source of income for the family. It is also possible that John Shakespeare—described by contemporaries as "merry cheeked"—may have developed an undue fondness for drink, leading to his downfall. Though undocumented, this possibility finds some support in Shakespeare's treatment of such characters as Falstaff and Sir Toby, which reveal a rich and often sympathetic appreciation for both the gaiety that heavy drink can provide, as well as the ensuing wastefulness that can result.

**Whether the opening play in the War of the Roses saga was Shakespeare's first attempt at drama is open to question. One might infer, from the jealousy of Robert Greene, that the cocky young man from Warwickshire had already enjoyed a measure of success for some time.

The Sonnets of William Shakespeare

Though the lack of available records obscures the early years of his career in London, Shakespeare ultimately became a shareholder in the theater company for which he was the principal playwright, and he purchased a holding in the Lord Chamberlain's Men when the company was formed in 1594. Over the years, the success of his plays brought riches and fame to himself and his company, and his growing wealth would help him restore the family fortune his father had lost due to a change in circumstances. Still, success was by no means assured. The plague had closed all the theaters for the summer season of 1592, and it appears that the promising poet's career was rescued by the young Earl of Southampton,[*] who not only supplied needed patronage for the emerging writer, but may have been the inspiration for many of the *Sonnets*. Success followed the reopening of the theaters, and the ensuing years brought artistic acclaim as well as commercial success. In 1594 *Richard III*, the last play in Shakespeare's War of the Roses tetralogy, opened to begin a remarkable run of profitability and artistic success that included history, drama, and comedy on a scale never seen before or since.[**] Two years later, in 1596, John Shakespeare was granted a coat of arms, obtaining the right for descendants—including his renowned and socially ambitious son, William—the right to be called a "gentleman."

Though all writers reflect the times around them, it is impossible to know with certainty when Shakespeare wrote his sonnets. Most

---

[*] Shakespeare's first venture into published poetry—*Venus and Adonis*, published in April, 1593—was dedicated to the young man, who was apparently the object of attention for a number of aspiring writers. In addition to attracting the sought-after patronage, it was also a resounding commercial success, resulting in the release of multiple editions during the author's lifetime.

[**] The two decades that comprised Shakespeare's life as an active playwright saw him average two new plays each year—usually one comedy and one tragedy—to add to his company's repertoire.

To sense the level of his accomplishment, today this would be roughly akin to Andrew Lloyd Webber writing and producing two new blockbuster plays each year for twenty years.

likely, he wrote them throughout his life, and the passages may reflect moods and circumstances that evolved with the times. A few may be traced to likely events—such as the death of Queen Elizabeth, which is one of several plausible explanations for the dire allusions teasingly presented in Sonnet 107. But comparing the historical record with production records for his plays can give us a sense of the times in which he was writing.

The plague that followed the opening play of the War of the Roses saga in 1592 killed more than 22,000 people. Shakespeare, meanwhile, would have been writing his War of the Roses plays in the late 1580s or early 1590s, while London was still teeming with soldiers: the Spanish Armada had only recently been defeated (in 1588), and armed conflict with Spain would continue until the death of Elizabeth in 1603, when her successor negotiated a peace. Soldiers, who populate many of Shakespeare's plays with characters ranging from noble and heroic to cowardly and shady, would have been everywhere during his most productive years.

In 1601, John Shakespeare died at the age of seventy, a decade after his famous son began to set the literary world on fire. His final illness and death may well be reflected in the brooding melancholy and dramatic impact of *Hamlet*—a play in which the protagonist is obsessed by his father's death, and which Shakespeare was writing in late 1600 and early 1601.* But the aftermath of *Hamlet* saw a new Shakespeare emerging—one at home with inward reflection, and infusing his work with an emotional power at which his earlier work, however brilliant, only hinted.

The plague returned to London in 1603, killing more than 30,000 people in the year that Elizabeth died, and James I took the throne. Though not without his eccentricities, James was a learned and highly educated man, who had studied under some of the greatest scholars of the day. The new king elevated Shakespeare's company to a special status as his own troupe of players, and granted them a

---

*Scholars have also speculated on the significance of the similarity in the name of the protagonist to Shakespeare's son, Hamnet—who died in 1596.

special patent that allowed them to travel throughout England during the plague year, performing at various cities around the country. During this same time, Shakespeare would have been writing *Othello*, which King James attended in 1604. The tragedy of *King Lear* followed soon thereafter—as did a reopening of witch-hunting season, a likely result of the new king's obsession with witchcraft, reflected in the Witchcraft Statute of 1604. Always trying to keep abreast of developing public tastes, Shakespeare responded by introducing the witches of *Macbeth* in 1606, at roughly the same time that Spain's greatest writer was nearing his own rendezvous with immortality.*

Edmund Shakepeare, William's younger brother, died in 1607; the year also saw the opening of *Anthony and Cleopatra* and *Timon of Athens*, as well as the founding of the Jamestown colony in modern Virginia. The following year, Shakespeare's mother passed away; it was the year that first saw *Pericles* and *Coriolanus*, as well as the appearance on the world stage of a young girl named Elizabeth Hall, the baby who was Shakespeare's first grandchild. And in 1609, the same year that Galileo built his first telescope, the *Sonnets* were first published, helping to ease Shakespeare into a semi-retirement that would still produce *Cybmeline*, *The Winter's Tale*, and *The Tempest*.

Elsewhere in the world, events were moving rapidly, changing the world in unforeseen and disturbing ways. Religious conflicts abounded, and war threatened England on every front. It was also a time of exploration and adventure. The New World was beckoning to the Old, and the age of Shakespeare was in many ways an age of possibilities. Pirates roamed the seas, and the Spanish were busy taking gold from their colonies. The French and Dutch were staking their claims in North America. And waves of English colonists were getting ready to sail: as the Jamestown colony was struggling to survive in early Virginia, the Pilgrims would land on Plymouth Rock—in 1620, four years after Shakespeare's death in 1616.

---

*Migel de Cervantes published *Don Quixote* in 1605.

Introduction

From Stratford to London

The market town of Stratford-upon-Avon in Warwickshire grew where a road (or *straet*) came to make a crossing (or ford) over the Avon River. In the Sixteenth Century it was the biggest village near Snittersfield, the ancestral home of the Shakespeares. And it was the town to which the ambitious but unlettered John Shakespeare migrated, seeking a better life as a tradesman in the glove-making trade. Travelers to the region noted its picturesque setting, nestled between the fertile valleys to the south and the forests to the north. Prosperous and growing, the town was home to a thousand or so inhabitants, a number that would vary with the effects of the plague.

London, by contrast, was a major metropolis of some 200,000 souls located on the Thames River, a major thoroughfare inland from the sea. London was small by modern standards, only a mile or so square, but enjoyed a number of special privileges. The Sovereign, though widely assumed to have been chosen by God Himself, could not enter town without an invitation. And athwart the Thames stood one of the then-modern wonders of the world: London Bridge, the only bridge spanning the river, which made London a strategic as well as a cultural center. The bridge was a marvel of modern construction and a popular destination for tourists, and its southern gate was often adorned with the severed heads of executed criminals.*

The city itself was filthy and crowded, even by the standards of the day. Houses were crowded together with no sewers or sanitation, except for the gutters running down the middle of the streets. Garbage and filth would simply lie where they were dumped until the next heavy rain. Then, the water would flush the gutters into the larger ditches, from which the stench could be smelled for miles. Human waste was usually collected in carts and hauled into the sea.

---

*Two of the traitors whose heads adorned London Bridge at the time Shakespeare arrived in London were likely distant relatives of his, on his mother's side, victims of religious turmoil in the days before the Spanish Armada met its fate in the stormy waters of the English Channel.

On the other hand, in the days of the Tudors London had no factory smoke to begrime the buildings, and the waters of the Thames flowed clear all the way to the sea. Outside town the mansions and gardens of the wealthy lined the river, and barges of nobles on holiday would move up and down the Thames.

The city itself was largely self-governing, or at least strived gamely in the attempt. A Lord Mayor, elected annually from among the Council of Aldermen, had his hands full trying to cope with the boisterous and often rowdy residents. The city was also growing: suburbs were sprouting to the north of town, under the separate jurisdiction of the County of Middlesex. Riots were common in city and suburb alike: with no regular police force to maintain order, a ready supply of rabble—including headstrong apprentices, ex-soldiers returning home, and a sea of unemployed men—stood eager and willing to vent their frustrations at the slightest provocation.

In contrast to life in the big city, country life was simple. Roads were terrible everywhere, encouraging people to stay put. Aside from farmers hauling their wares to town, and men of wealth showing off their elegant and expensive, though utterly springless coaches, traffic on the roads consisted mostly of horses or people walking on foot. The weekly market day in the nearest town, and the annual fairs in the larger cities, provided the chance to exchange goods, as well as the latest news. Communications, however, were otherwise as bad as the roads. Travelers were expected to report whatever they had seen or heard, and most people had to rely upon hearsay and gossip for the latest news.

Virtually unknown today, the Bubonic Plague was a major health problem in Elizabethan England, a result of overcrowding and poor sanitation. Though powerless to stop it, some medical radicals saw a link between disease and the filth of Sixteenth Century life. Most, however, viewed the plague as a sign of God's displeasure, though there were the usual disagreements about who was provoking heaven's wrath. Dogs and cats were often viewed as carriers of the plague, and during an outbreak were often killed in large numbers;

this, in turn, would lead to an increase in the rat population—which, breeding in the filth and squalor, carried the fleas that carried the actual plague.

Crime and Punishment

Though our own legal heritage owes much to the English common law, today's concept of "law and order" differs markedly from the laws that Shakespeare would have known. These were, after all, the days of the Spanish Inquisition, where heretics and witches were burned at the stake. Unsurprisingly, the Elizabethan system of criminal justice was, by modern standards, barbaric. Serious crimes were punishable by death, and public executions—particularly hangings, drawings and quarterings, and the burning alive of heretics and other dangerous non-conformists—were enjoyed as spectacles.

While there were no police departments in the modern sense of the word, upon the "hue and cry" that some crime had been discovered, the entire community would participate in chasing down and catching the wretched offender. Since communities were small there were few places to hide, and strangers were always regarded with suspicion. Escape was not easy, and once captured, the accused would face English justice.*

The right to counsel being unknown at common law, most defendants were at the mercy of their prosecutors, and had to rely upon the integrity of the court to avoid being executed by mistake. The fortunate felon who happened to be literate, however, could plead "benefit of clergy"—invoking, through his ability to read, the polite fiction that he was entitled to treatment due members of the

---

*There were, however, many practical problems with enforcement—most notably the fact that in a system with no permanent police force, the entire system depended on the services of amateurs, and prosecution was often a time-consuming and troublesome endeavor. As a result, many petty crimes would go unpunished, and the local justices and prosecutors—who would have to live with the results of any action they undertook, to the likely detriment of their own livelihood if their brand of justice proved too stern for local tastes—usually preferred less formal means of resolving disputes.

clergy, thereby transferring his case to the ecclesiastical courts which lacked the jurisdiction to hang the offender. Instead, after being branded with a reminder of his crime, the fortunate thief or murderer would be sent on his way with an admonition to repent.*

Beheading was a punishment reserved for nobles and gentlemen of high standing, and ordinary citizens were put to death in ways intended to warn others against the evil ways of wickedness. Accordingly, wives who poisoned their husbands would be burned at the stake, but the most common form of execution was hanging—an event which usually drew a large crowd of spectators. Those guilty of treason, however, faced less gentle treatment, and would be hung, drawn, and quartered: strung up by his neck, the condemned would be cut down from the noose just before falling unconscious. For an encore, he would be slit open and have his entrails drawn out and burned before his eyes, usually to the merriment of the crowd; then his body would be dismembered—perhaps dipped into boiling tar to add some seasoning—and various bits and pieces would be displayed throughout the city.**

Because a conviction for felony or treason carried with it the forfeiture of the offender's assets to the crown, avoiding a conviction carried advantages—if not to the accused, then to his family, who might otherwise become destitute and stripped of all entitlements. Since the law of the day required a plea of "guilty" or "not

---

*This legal plea worked only once, however. Even the ecclesiastics had a limit to their patience, and a second offense could prove to be as fatal as the first one would be for the illiterate rabble.

On the other hand, large numbers of those convicted managed to secure the benefit of this live-saving plea—perhaps assisted by the fact that they would be asked to read a verse of scripture (invariably a verse from Psalm 51, which came to be known as the "neck verse") that they could have memorized. And many juries and judges would deliberately undervalue the worth of any goods the defendant may have stolen, thereby converting a felony—punishable by death—into a petty misdemeanor, punishable by a fine and a whipping.

**The fortunate traitor, if he comported himself with courage and aplomb, might be allowed to hang until he was actually dead.

guilty" to allow a trial to proceed, a defendant hoping to escape judgment would simply refuse to enter any plea at all—"standing dumb at the bar," as the term was used—and thereby avoid a conviction. To discourage such an unprofitable turn of events, the law employed a sanction known as *peine forte et dure*—or, pressing to death—to encourage a plea: the authorities would stretch the defendant out upon a bed of spikes, his legs and arms extended, and a board would be laid on top of him, with increasing weights added until he changed his mind. Or was crushed to death.*

At the other end of the criminal spectrum, petty crimes included vagrancy, petty theft, assaults, non-attendance at church services, and running afoul of the various regulatory statutes that Parliament took into its head to pass from time to time. Among the latter were attempts to close down the many unlicensed alehouses that were constantly springing up throughout the country. Such efforts were, in large part, spearheaded by the moralists of the day, who worried about the moral decline of servants straying outside their masters' supervision and found it inexcusable for villagers to be wasting their Sundays reveling, instead of keeping the Sabbath by going to church. Though occasionally successful, these campaigns tended to founder on the gossip and ridicule that invariably attended efforts by local officials to enforce these particular laws. As a result, whenever possible local officials preferred to ignore crimes that, in their view, had no victim. And to keep peace within their own community, officials preferred mediation between the affected parties to the draconian sanctions available at law.

Education
By the time of Elizabeth, the Renaissance was well underway, and the English were well acquainted with the value of a good education. Most men of social prominence were literate, and many were quite

---

*Though it might shock the Elizabethans' sense of moral justice, the more permissive courts of today regard "standing mute" as the equivalent of pleading "not guilty."

cultured. Throughout the country, businessmen were funneling money into schools, hoping to create a workforce educated and advanced enough to deal with the rapid pace of change afoot in the world. Universities were available for the gifted or well-connected, but the supply of promising young scholars always exceeded the number of places available, and the religious turmoil of the day often placed further restrictions on those of Catholic upbringing. As ever, the curious and thoughtful could find themselves at a disadvantage in the scramble to make a living, for aside from the well-to-do, few had the time or resources to ponder the eternal questions of existence to their heart's content. But along with his father's social prominence and growing personal wealth, Shakespeare had the advantage of a series of highly accomplished teachers, drawn to Stratford by the relatively high pay and rent-free lodging furnished to the local schoolmaster.

For a young schoolboy,* education began at the age of five, when the students were charged with mastering the alphabet, along with the common catechism of the day. The school day was a long one—normally eight hours or longer, starting early in the morning and extending until the late afternoon. Much time would be spent mastering Latin grammar and composition. Older students would study many of the ancient classics, including works by Virgil, Ovid, and Cicero. Significantly for the course of English literature, the Stratford schoolmasters of Shakespeare's day included several who placed particular emphasis on the use of eloquence and drama in teaching the curriculum. In addition, touring companies of players frequently staged performances in and around Stratford during his formative years, adding a touch of pageantry to what would, by today's standards, be a challenging course of study for any young man in any era.

---

*At the time, "schoolgirls" would have been a largely unfamiliar concept: for all intents and purposes, though the English of the day were ruled by a Queen and were not opposed in principle to the education of females, the system was not open to girls.

Introduction

Some skeptics, disdaining the limited education that Shakespeare received, claim that his lack of a proper university education proves that someone else wrote the works that bear his name. However, the fact remains that schoolboys of the era received an education more steeped in the classics than most students receive in our own time. And the records show that few of Shakespeare's classmates continued on to a full, formal university education. If young Will Shakespeare had joined them, he may well have attained the literary pedigree that would have convinced later academics that he was, indeed, one of them—but might, in return, have lost much of the inventiveness that made his works so powerful and fresh to his audiences. But his education and surroundings would have given him all the tools he needed to move into the larger world around him; his adventurous spirit and inquisitive mind were what propelled him to greatness.*

Ye Olde Entertainmente Industrie

By the Sixteenth Century, technology was already beginning its inexorable advance. Modern innovations such as movable type and the printing press were making their presence felt everywhere, including England. Booksellers abounded, and every year saw new publications appear at the booksellers—books on religion and history, as well as novels and poetry. Predictably, much of it was dreadful: in Shakespeare's day, as in our own, the public's demand for diversions and entertainment far exceeded the capacity of gifted artists to produce, and the supply ranged from the scurrilous to the sublime. Soon after the invention of the printing press the State imposed controls, to guard against the issuance of disgraceful or seditious publications. Regulations abounded, but were often overlooked until some scandalous book appeared. Then, the authorities would mount an inquiry, and the rules would be scrupulously enforced until the matter could be discreetly forgotten.

---

*See, Kay, *Shakespeare,* pp 39-52 for a more detailed account of likely course of Shakespeare's early education.

While the system of rules and regulations complicated efforts to publish anything seriously seditious, it was easy enough to print and distribute flyers on a single sheet of paper. And a common way of ruffling the feathers of those in power was to go wandering around town singing rude or bawdy songs about them.

As a young man entering London from the countryside, Shakespeare would have faced both daunting challenges and tantalizing opportunities. London was bursting at the seams, and the young man from Stratford seemed to have inherited both his father's sense of adventure and determination to make a name for himself. Whether he came after joining a troupe of actors, or moved to the big city to seek his fortune, the upheaval in his life would have been both exciting and frightening.* But if he also inherited his father's head for business, he would have sensed the rich commercial prospects that lay in feeding the public's growing hunger for entertainment—a hunger fed by festivals and plays, as well as bear-baiting, games and sports of various kinds, and public executions. As the young player grew to realize the scope of his abilities as an actor and writer, he would have realized that anything was possible.

Still, Shakespeare's chosen profession presented him with more than its share of problems. The theater itself was a new innovation in public entertainment. Though touring companies of players were well-known in his day, the fixed theater was an artistic development that did not exist at Shakespeare's birth. Ominously, the theater was always skirting the unwelcome attention of preachers and other moralists. These guardians of public decency were appalled at the thought of common people enjoying themselves, and outraged that a public which had such problems sitting through a one-hour sermon could sit, joyously enraptured, for hours at the playhouse.

---

*It is likely that the young Shakespeare would have had some connections to follow into London: his father was, after all, a country merchant of some repute; and a statute passed by Parliament imposed severe penalties upon "common players...and minstrels" unless they were under the patronage of a noble, or duly licensed—deeming them to be "rogues, vagabonds, and sturdy beggars." See, Kay, *Shakespeare*, pp 71-95.

Introduction

Some of Shakespeare's sonnets reflect the fact that his background in the theater marked him as one from a not-quite-reputable profession. And it was a profession in constant need of patrons, for by practicing a trade which was associated with vagrants, vagabonds, and others without an honest livelihood, acting troupes unable to posture as servants of some respectable household were subject to arrest and punishment.* Depending upon the upper classes for protection, they had a continuing incentive not to antagonize their patrons, and to portray the upper crust in ways complimentary enough to continue their sponsorship. But Shakespeare had the unique gift of being able to delight audiences comprised of all classes—deflating the pompous, to the delight of the masses, while at the same time representing nobility of spirit as a human quality often associated with nobility of rank. Shakespeare also kept a watchful eye on public tastes, and his plays—which even today spring to life in live performance—reflect a playwright with a keen sense of what will play well to an audience. It was a delicate balancing act, and one which he was constantly refining.

Unfortunately, not all of the problems were amenable to the wit and artistry of the playwright. In 1598, for example, the need for a stage nearly shut down his production company during a dispute over the lease for the theater on which they performed. The solution was to dismantle the one theater—which was technically legal, since they owned the structure, though not the land on which it sat—and build another, which they called the Globe. In addition, plague epidemics often complicated production schedules—and touring troupes of players were common, particularly when needs of public health prevented large groups from gathering in the City. Many of these traditions survive in London's theater district to this day—playhouses and open air theaters being among the earliest forms of mass entertainment on a grand scale.

---

*Needing to portray the nobility as well as the common people, actors were entitled to own clothing suited to the upper classes—unlike most of their class, who were expected to dress appropriately to their station in life.

The Sonnets of William Shakespeare

Politics and Religion

Although education and literacy were making great strides in sixteenth century England, religious turmoil and superstition were widespread and pervasive. Witchcraft was often a more comforting explanation for misfortune than the judgment of God upon a sinner, and so the Witchcraft Statute of 1604 was an effort to stop its diabolical effects, even as resort to counter-magic was sometimes seen as the most effective recourse against a run of bad luck.* Against this backdrop, the upheaval of the Reformation, beginning in England with Henry VIII's break from the Roman Catholic Church, worked a profound effect upon English society.

Religion and patriotism are said to be refuges of scoundrels, and in the days of the Reformation sectarian differences provided easy justifications for self-interest disguised as piety. Nations with conflicting ambitions needed to look no further than the obvious heresy of their natural enemies to justify taking action. And England, seen as having been led astray by the strong-willed Henry VIII, was a convenient target for enemies, without and within. Sectarian strife within England soon left her divided at home, and with few friends abroad.

---

*Parliament passed the Witchcraft Statute a year after the ascension of King James I to the throne following the death of Queen Elizabeth in 1603.

In point of fact, King James I was intensely interested in the subject of witchcraft, publishing a work on the subject in 1597 entitled *Daemonologie*—in which the future king refuted skeptics of the day by showing how disbelief in witchcraft was a step in the direction of damnation and atheism. As king, he ordered copies of a leading skeptic's book—Reginald Scot's *The Discovery of Witchcraft*, published in 1584, warning against the hysteria that caused otherwise rational people to torture and burn their innocent fellow creatures—to be burned, as well.

Oddly enough, witchcraft—usually resulting in a diseased cow, a dead child, an otherwise inexplicable case of impotence, or some other supernatural calamity—seemed to be practiced largely by ugly, crabby, and defenseless old women living in poverty-stricken shacks on the edge of town. Occasionally, though, suspicions would be aroused by a woman who seemed to possess an unusual or unnatural gift for healing the sick. In any case, most accused witches denied their guilt stubbornly, confessing only under the persuasive power of torture.

Introduction

By the time Elizabeth took the throne, England was weary of the internal discord. The Queen, too practical to be a zealot where religion was concerned, showed little interest in parsing the intricacies of then-current theology, and the law establishing the Church of England was largely an attempt to end the religious schisms that had plagued her country. These schisms were made all the more bitter because King Henry, in his break with Rome, had made a point of dispersing the accumulated riches of the Church among various groups of his followers, who had little interest in giving them back. For the most part, the country quickly accepted the change, eager to put the bitterness of the past behind them.

Inevitably, the political compromise failed to satisfy the various zealots on all sides. Shakespeare's own cousin was put to death in 1583, during a reprise of sectarian strife. Some religious dissidents turned violent—such as those who plotted the overthrow and murder of the Queen in order to restore the supremacy of Rome.* Others, like the Puritans, simply demanded wide-ranging reforms that, if adopted, would have carried the added benefit of forcing everyone else to adhere to their particular views of the Supreme Being. As in our own day, many of these doctrinal differences were less significant than the political differences that each side sought to advance—with the odd coincidence, then as always, that God invariably seemed to share the world view of whichever side was calling upon heaven to help its own particular cause. And as today, many seeking reform of their society sought to root their economic or political theories not on the teachings of science, but on the most convenient passages of the Scriptures.

By the 1590s, some measure of the freedom of thought and expression that marked the Renaissance had returned to England. Even so, the threat of persecution took a long time to fade, and the

---

* As was the case with witches, many of the convictions and ensuing executions of admitted traitors relied upon the confessions of the accused. These confessions were assisted, as necessary, by the liberal use of various and highly persuasive forms of torture, which were often administered by those with a vested interest in the outcome of a particular interrogation.

shadows lasted long enough to send the Pilgrims and others on their way to the New World in search of religious and political liberty.* In fact, Shakespeare's connection to patrons connected to a doomed attempted *coup d'etat* near the turn of the century could have made his own position at court precarious, if not for his masterful ability to transcend politics in his writing.** In this, he exhibited a gift for tactfully weaving compelling and captivating tales out of the conflicting interests, passions, and humanity of the characters in his plays, at once relating their actions to matters of topical interest to his audience while managing to avoid the meddlesome attentions of the censors.

Politically, the monarch was the head of state, much as Elizabethan society viewed the father as the head of the family. Elizabeth, widely viewed as among the greatest monarchs in English history, took her responsibilities seriously, and deemed herself bound to her subjects by the same God that had chosen her to lead them. As a result, she took a keen interest in all aspects of her government. Her government relied upon a Privy Council, consisting of her ministers of state to carry out her policies.

English society was highly stratified, and all were expected to show proper deference to their social superiors. The English nobility—consisting in Shakespeare's days of dukes, earls, viscounts, and barons—resulted from a document called a patent, given by the sovereign and embossed by the Great Seal of England. This document conferred an inheritable title of honor that descended to

---

*As our own early history attests, having suffered through persecution themselves, many religious dissidents were only too eager to return the favor when they gained the upper hand.

**The day before the attempted rebellion, there was a performance of *Richard II*—a play about a irresolute and unfit monarch confronted by an intrepid opponent—at the Globe Theater, before an audience comprised of many of the insurrectionists, possibly including Shakespeare's patron, the Earl of Southampton. Had the authorities chosen to believe that the players were sympathizers, English literary history might have taken a different course. See, Kay, *Shakespeare*, pp 264-266 for an account of the incident.

the eldest son. Nobles typically enjoyed many high privileges—estates, servants, and special privileges at court. In return, they could be called upon as needed to serve the State. Commoners—including, at times, members of the Privy Council—could be promoted to the nobility for service to the crown. Today, a vestige of this heritage survives in the British House of Lords.

Knighthood, a title meant to confer honors for any number of purposes, bestowed a non-hereditary rank upon its recipient. Knights—who carried the title "Sir" before their names—ranked below the nobility in the Elizabethan pecking order.

A proper Elizabethan "gentleman" became one not by showing proper manners, but by receiving a coat of arms from the College of Heralds. The requirements were simply good birth and independent means—or, in other words, being a non-bastard who did not need unseemly employment in a trade or profession. Gentlemen were expected to engage freely in public service and other good works. But as in any society, rich people with time on their hands were often tempted to less savory pursuits, providing scandals for the amusement of all. After earlier efforts had met with little success—most likely owing to the change in the family's financial circumstances—Shakespeare's father had his application for a coat of arms approved in 1596, undoubtedly at the instance of his now-famous son, who was by then wealthy enough, and moving in circles lofty enough, to wield some influence in the halls of power.*

---

*Actually, the redemption of his father carried benefits for his now-prominent and socially ambitious son, whose standing in society would have been enhanced by the elevation of his father. As a result, Shakespeare may have had additional motives for renewing his father's application for a coat of arms, besides simply wanting to do something nice for his dad.

Sadly, the honor bestowed on his father came two months after the funeral of Shakespeare's son 11-year old, Hamnet—who would have inherited the title "gentleman" from his famous father. On a human level, we are left to speculate on the bittersweet turn in the family fortunes—for in addition to the redemption of John Shakespeare and the death of his grandson, the year 1596 was most likely the year Shakespeare was working on *King John* and *The Merchant of Venice*.

After the nobles and gentry, citizens and burgesses—marked by their trades and their cities, and eligible for service in public office—enjoyed a rank above the yeoman of the countryside, who either possessed their own land or farmed a gentleman's estate. And at the bottom of the ladder came the common laborers and servants—who, though doing most of the work, had little power and no real wealth. Women and children typically had no independent rank, deriving their station in life from that of their husband or father. There was, however, the real possibility of movement between ranks, providing an element of social and economic dynamism among the talented and ambitious that served to underscore and enforce the social order, rather than to undercut it.

Love & Romance

With the primitive roads, and communications between different parts of the country largely reduced to rumor, it is not surprising that most people seldom ventured far from home. As a result, marriages were usually between a man and woman who had grown up together, and settled close to where they were born.

The first step toward marriage was usually a betrothal—a private affair between a man and woman that often carried many of the same fringe benefits as marriage. Formal banns would be published in the local church, with the minister publically announcing the couple's intentions, and calling upon anyone having information casting the lawfulness of the marriage into doubt to come forward.*

In all cultures, weddings give everyone a reason to celebrate—and Elizabethan England, with its lust for festivals and feasts, was no exception. Weddings were usually all-day affairs, beginning in at the bride's home, where the groom and assembled friends and musicians would gather early in the day for the procession to the local church. After the formal ceremony, everyone would hurry to

---

*Of course, as in any era, some couples had to expedite things—occasionally to accommodate an anticipated departure, more often to accommodate an unexpected arrival. Couples needing to hasten their marriage could get a special dispensation from the bishop.

the groom's house for the wedding feast—spending the rest of the day eating, drinking, and enjoying various forms of entertainment.

Predictably, as the revelers reveled, the party would become rowdier and more rambunctious until, finally, the bride and groom would be led to the wedding chamber. The bride would usually be undressed by her bridesmaids—the groom by his groomsmen—and the couple would typically find themselves sewn into their bedsheets amid the taunting and laughter of their by-now thoroughly besotted friends. Having accomplished their intended purpose, these friends would leave the couple alone and go back to the party, returning to serenade the couple the following morning.

Beneath the happy picture of domestic contentment, of course, each era suffers its own problems and limitations. As artistically and emotionally powerful as in any era, a woman in Shakespeare's day enjoyed few legal rights, and upon marriage her husband assumed control over her property and possessions. In addition, "betrothals" made before witnesses were viewed as binding contracts of marriage. This made abuse and fraud both predictable and inevitable— particularly where the wealthy or naive were involved—and courts were often called upon to settle a wide range of disputes.

Under law and custom, a father was deemed the master of his house, and could marry off his daughters as he saw fit. Still, few parents sought to arrange marriages that condemned their children to lives of unending woe, and most tried to find matches that took into account the hopes and desires of their children. But these were also times where family blood lines were guarded jealously, and marriage was often seen as a way of resolving conflicts or cementing alliances. Consequently, relations among well-to-do family members were often practical, and sometimes devoid of sentiment. Parents ruled their children, and the good son or daughter was respectful in return. As a result, while the hearts of Elizabethans coursed as strongly with affection toward the opposite sex as those of any era, romantic love was not encouraged. Marriages were, in essence, a practical union of households; and as the primary purpose was to raise children and increase the family's estate, little room was left for tenderness—at least, within the formal structure of the cultured family. And so dalliances abounded, and much Elizabethan humor revolved around "cuckolds"—husbands deceived by faithless wives and their paramours into raising the lover's child as his own.

Proper Elizabethan ladies were expected to be obedient and attentive to the needs of their husbands, and those who were married to men of high rank and station may well have had ample reason to do so.* As ever, the wives of powerful men were often quite a bit younger than their husbands, and their youthful inexperience with the ways of the world—combined with the influence of their own parents, who were likely responsible for arranging the match and eager to see it succeed—may have given them an incentive to follow the path of least resistence, and defer to their husbands when they could.

As in our day, there was a great divide between the wealthy elite and the common folk in many areas, and love was no exception. While records of the upper class follow classical domestic conventions, diaries and records from their social inferiors disclose a family life that—at least in the accounts of marital discords and squabbles—seems almost modern. "God knows what I should do," wrote one perplexed husband, in terms familiar to married men before and since:

> These four years have I now lived with her, and do not know how to humour her. When she is angry, I do aggravate her passion by saying anything....When she is patient, [the] peace is so sweet to me that I dare not speak lest I should lose it.**

---

*Or, at least to maintain the appearance of doing so.

**Wrightson, *English Society 1580-1680* (1985), pp 95-96. Squabbling between the sexes may, it seems, transcend boundaries of time and culture.

Of course, most women had no access to education in Shakespeare's day, or were discreet about committing their opinions of the men around them to paper. Typically, we are left with only the husband's accounts of family life.

Introduction

With fewer worries about class status and property to concern them, many marriages among the common folk were matches made for love, rather than for reasons of financial, political, or social alliance. Relationships also tended to be more practical—and, quite likely, richer in non-material ways—among those less encumbered by wealth or status. Upper-class women were often seen more as possessions than partners, to be displayed or cast aside, depending on the needs of the lord of the manor. Among common folk, marriage was likely to be a partnership born of emotional and practical necessity, in which the woman would feel freer to assert herself—and risked less from the displeasure of her husband who, after all, relied on her for help as well as companionship.

Marriage was, in the sixteenth century, deemed to be forever, and divorce was virtually unknown.* When arranging a marriage for their children, parents typically took care to ensure as optimum a match as possible—seeking a mate for their child who was compatible in terms of wealth, social standing, morality, and religion. A level of personal compatibility was desirable but was not deemed essential. But as always, matches arranged between the young people themselves tended to focus on love—often ignoring the better judgment of their elders.**

Marriage was also, in Shakespeare's day, commonly deemed to occur upon betrothal—and a young couple in love, formally

---

*Unless, perhaps, the husband was the King of England—who established his authority to rewrite the rules on marriage over the dead bodies of dissenting clerics...and some of his unfortunate wives.

**Inevitably, youthful lust played its usual role in self-arranged marriages as well. Shakespeare himself, for example, married a woman eight years his senior—six months before the birth of their first child.

One does not know the reaction of the families, but many of Shakespeare's plays reflect a theme of delaying sexual gratification until after a formal marriage: Romeo and Juliet, for example, did not consummate their passion for each other until their nuptials were behind them. We cannot be sure whether this reflects a bow to conventional morality, or a playwright reflecting on his own youthful follies.

committed to marry, often consummated their relationship well in advance of the nuptials. The inevitable result was that English brides were often pregnant on their wedding day. Unfortunately, as in any age, the men in Shakespeare's day were not always honorable, and occasionally the betrothed and pregnant bride was abandoned by a lover who preferred to flee rather than settle down and raise a family. Poor girls, in particular, were vulnerable to the wiles and charms of ardent suitors, and if they misjudged the intentions of their intended they would be left alone to face the consequences.* The unlucky girl, faced with giving birth to a bastard child, often faced a wide range of punishment and scorn—including dismissal from her place of service; possible imprisonment, if the local authorities deemed her to pose the risk of letting her child become a burden on the parish; and denial of a midwife's assistance at birth unless she identified the father. Some terrified girls, faced with the shame and hardship of bearing a bastard child, would take efforts to conceal their pregnancy, and abandon their baby to the elements—or simply kill the child upon birth. Others simply endured as best they could, with themselves and their children sacrificed to uphold the English principle of family formation: that children should be born and raised within an intact and economically independent nuclear family.**

Though much of his writing reflected conventional notions of morality, Shakespeare appears to have lived apart from his wife and children for most of his life, preferring to live close to his work in London. He appears to have been in constant contact, however, and in 1597 he purchased one of the nicest houses in Stratford, called New Place, as a home for his family. But his relationship with his wife is the subject of controversy: he did, after all, leave her with three small children in the 1580s to move to London; and his will

---

*As in most eras, the consequences flowing from illegitimacy tended to fall unevenly: fathers, if found, typically faced no more than penance and an order of maintenance.

**Wrightson, *English Society 1580-1680* (1982), pp 85-86.

mentions her only to leave her his "second best bed." This leads many to speculate that the relationship was a chilly one. If so, many of his tenderest sonnets—as well as the lofty passages on love appearing in many of his plays—may have expressed his longing in his art for the love he could not find in his life. On the other hand, the bawdiness of his plays and sonnets suggests that he was not the kind to spend his life pining over a love that turned out badly; and whether the "second best bed" was a slap at his wife, as many suppose—or a last remembrance, trusting that the daughter to whom he was leaving the bulk of his estate would be sure to tend after her mother—we cannot know for certain. The mention of his wife would, however, have ensured that the will could not be challenged on grounds that he forgot to make a provision for her; and some of his dealings in the last years of his life make sense only if he was trying to insulate his business partners from any claim by his wife on any jointly-held business property.

In any case, Shakespeare left us surprisingly little of his personal joy or anguish: we have no correspondence between himself and his family to give us insight into his private relationships with his wife and children—no heartfelt farewells, nor even any thoughts on the death of his eleven-year old son Hamnet in 1596. His last will and testament did not read like Anthony's funeral oration: it was lawyerly and sterile, intended to transfer property and not to stir the souls of men. And so the man who wrote so beautifully of love appears, in the end, to have revealed his passion through his writing—which did not include any tender words expressed to those closest to him. Whether this reflects words unwritten due to the quick onset of death, or a void in his life that he could only fill through his art, we will never know.

Notes on Shakespeare's Sonnets:

As with Shakespeare's life, the facts surrounding his sonnets are sketchy at best, encouraging theories about them to flourish. The first mention of them—a passing reference to the "honey-tongued Shakespeare" and his "sugared sonnets" in Francis Meres' *Palladis*

Tamia in 1598—suggests that many were written during his early years as a playwright in the 1590s, and two were published separately in *The Passionate Pilgrim* in 1599. The sonnets in this volume are taken from the 1609 Quarto, which was published during Shakespeare's lifetime, though the author's participation or approval of the release is open to dispute. Subsequent versions—including releases in 1640 and 1709—generally follow the arrangement of the initial offering, but controversies abound. The arguments range from the usual disputes over authorship, to their "intended order," and include speculation of all sorts over whether they portray some sort of internal narrative, as well as the identity of the "principals"—the "fair youth," the "dark lady," and the various rival poets who appear to have been competing for the attention of the patron who was the subject of many of the poems. Often lost in the swirling controversies are the poems themselves, which show a different side of Shakespeare than we see in his plays. The dramatist was, after all, writing for dramatic effect and entertainment, and displays a remarkable range of insights into all manner of humanity. The *Sonnets*, by contrast, reflect a less heroic and more reflective temperament—alternatively sweet and bombastic, tender and taunting, but conveying a soft emotional honesty and a gentleness of spirit that is often quite touching.

In his plays as well as his poetry, Shakespeare is remarkably adept at reordering conventional notions of word order to achieve his matchless expression of ideas. Though some arrangements are obviously the result of searching for a rhyme needed to fit the pattern, the result is rarely forced, resulting in some of the loveliest, tenderest, and most personal verses known to English literature.

The fourteen-line sonnet was a fashionable art form in Elizabethan times, enjoying popularity throughout Europe. Shakespeare chose to use the English form of the sonnet—three four-line quatrains, followed by a couplet—rather than the Italian form, which utilized an octave, or eight-line grouping, followed by a six-line sestet. While both forms were highly structured, and called for a high level of skill by the poet, the English form appears to have

Introduction

allowed Shakespeare an infinite flexibility of expression. While the themes and images of most sonnets follow the divisions suggested by the format, his chosen form let him resolve or continue his themes as the subject (or the metrical needs of the iambic pentameter) struck him, often continuing his thoughts through the quatrain division.* Most editors, in fact, continue to use the form to guide their choice of modernized punctuation, reasoning that each quatrain usually marks the end of a completed thought.

Many sonnets are linked together, often by imagery or theme. Those which are obvious continuations of others are noted in the text. Even so, the order of the sonnets is, at times, hopelessly confused. Their original publication released them in what appears to be a less-than-coherent manner. In addition, they were apparently written over a long period of time, making assumptions about their subjects largely a matter of conjecture.

Despite the speculation of modern scholars, it is doubtful that Shakespeare intended his *Sonnets* to form a unified narrative. He may well have regarded narrative as better suited to his plays and narrative verse, and regarded his sonnets simply as poems. If so, some scholars may be placing emphasis where it does not belong—for if they were, in fact, written over a course of years and inspired by a number of different sources, our efforts to find coherence in their arrangement, or clues about the author in their structure, may simply be chasing after phantoms.

It is entirely possible that Shakespeare the Poet composed his *Sonnets* simply as inspiration struck, or to while away the time between other pursuits, If so, any attempt to discern a theme or narrative will be the product of our own imagination, and an all-too-human desire to impose order out of chaos. If we accept the fact that the author was a successful playwright and businessman, as well

---

*In addition, some departures from form may be the result of oversight: Sonnet 99, for example, contains fifteen lines, while Sonnet 126 contains twelve. And one verse—Sonnet 145, consisting of four iams, rather than five, and widely regarded as the weakest verse in the collection—may show an early effort by a poet who had not achieved the maturity of style that marked his later work.

as a gifted poet, it seems doubtful that there would have been any order or overarching theme to the collection as a whole when he was writing. It is, therefore, quite likely that he wrote sonnets when the mood struck him or a patron's request imposed upon him, and the available time allowed—after which he simply moved on to other things. However, the subjective "feel" of the poetry, the vulnerability and range of emotions conveyed in the sonnets—as well as the fact that they were written for private enjoyment, rather than for widespread distribution—suggests that some of them may well have been deeply personal, and may reflect events or personal relationships between Shakespeare and those close to him that are lost to time. Many, in fact, seem aimed at his own inner soul, permitting us to catch glimpses of the artist in his most private, most vulnerable moments—whether he finds himself "in disgrace with fortune and men's eyes"* or chastising himself for his lustful obsession with the "dark lady" of the later sonnets, where his passions find him "anchored in the bay where all men ride."**

In any case, the immortal dramatist who brought us *Hamlet* and *Macbeth* was capable of just as wide a range of emotive and evocative poetry in his sonnets as in his plays. The writer gently observing in Sonnet 116 that love

> ...is an ever fixèd mark
> That looks on tempests and is never shaken;
> It is the star to every wand'ring bark
> Whose worth's unknown, though his height be taken

speaks not of lustful passion, but of the serene contentment of mingling souls and shared dreams. Yet this is the same poet who wrote of passion leading to ruin or high farce in any number of plays. And the poet was no naive fool, and was fully aware that "loves best habit is in seeming trust," even if mutual happiness

---

*Sonnet 29.

**Sonnet 137.

sometimes depends on "simple truth suppressed,"* for cruelty under the flag of honesty is not the way of lovers. The same wry wit that brought us *Twelfth Night*—where love flows from disguise and misunderstanding—fully realized that it was "better to be vile than vile esteemed,"** particularly when the latter brings all the shame but none of the pleasures. Yet the *Sonnets* often portray a soul torn between pleasure and pain—a torment which is, in the end, often the by-product of the author's expressed sense of failure and inadequacy. And hidden among the beauty of the words are the bawdy puns and playful teasing, showing that the poet, whatever the momentary state of his emotions, can still laugh at life through any heartaches that it may bring his way—fully aware of all the humorous contradictions in that most human of organs, the heart.

Stylistically, Shakespeare's sonnets are more highly structured than the verse of his plays, requiring a different use of language to condense meaning to fit the form. Thoughts are often fragments, rather than fully developed themes, and many are continued into the next verse to complete his poetic idea. Moreover, while his plays were meant to be performed—and likely written and rewritten to suit the available company of actors and their looming performance deadlines, as well as the whims of the royal censors—it is likely that the *Sonnets* were carefully crafted, and meant to be read and reflected upon privately. While touching upon themes of friendship, affection, and love, they convey private emotions and among the most intimate expressions of the poet's mind, much like a letter in verse, revealing the poet's innermost thoughts—though tantalizingly concealing the identity of any of the subjects, through the translucent sheen of poetry.

Conventionally, sonnets reflected the predicament of a poet thwarted from access to an idealized object of his affections. The poet may also tantalize the reader through hints that the poems

---

*Sonnet 138.

**Sonnet 121.

reflect actual events—though Shakespeare was too inventive an artist for us to presume that they invariably reflect his life, rather than his artistry. Commonly, sonnets portray the poet as a wretched and rejected lover, torn by conflicting emotions of passion and idealized love. In Shakespeare, the sonnets often convey contending impulses as well, portraying the world as a contrast between beauty and cold reality, hope and despair. The highly structured form required discipline and creativity to let the poet achieve a unique voice. From its internal conflict and divisions the poet would explore his innermost self, in much the same way that the soliloquy of an actor would reveal the soul of a character on the stage.

Shakespeare was nothing if not original, and he showed a remarkable capacity to reinvent the familiar and turn it into something new. His *Sonnets*—like much of his other writing—often broke with established convention. The "dark lady" sonnets, for example, bear no relation to the ideal mistress of typical sonneteer pining, but is portrayed as lusty, sullen, and often cruel. Many sonnets are directed to a young man—possibly a patron, or patron's son, whom the poet is scolding for selfishly keeping his charms to himself, rather than finding a wife and reproducing. Some appear to reflect the relationship of patron to petitioner, dressed in the verbiage of the day and clad in the language of love. Clusters of them are related by theme or imagery, and while some appear to contain the seeds of a narrative thread—leading some to speculate that they track events in the author's life, if only we can uncover the players involved and crack the literary code—many appear to reflect a writer's exuberance for his times and his language, with little relation to the rest. For the literary sleuth, the promise of unraveling the mystery has kept controversy swirling around the sonnets since their publication in 1609. For the rest of us, there is enough warmth and human passion in the poems to allow the reader to enjoy them without the need to hunt for ulterior motives.

Today, we often capitalize concepts such as Time and Beauty to vest each with an almost anthropomorphic existence—Father Time, as opposed to time passing on a clock. In Shakespeare's day the rules on capitalization, like those on punctuation and spelling, were unstandardized and verged on the chaotic. Nouns were often capitalized for no particular reason other than doing so happened to strike the writer's fancy on a given day. And since the rules of conventional spelling and punctuation were still some years in the future, it is misleading to read too much into Shakespeare's choices.* Therefore, though purists may shudder (even if the casual reader may never notice), in an effort to make them less obscure or intimidating, the *Sonnets* in this edition come complete with conventional Americanized spelling and a modest attempt at modernized punctuation. They do, however, include some stress marks, where the constraints imposed by the sonnet form might otherwise break the flow of the meter. And where the text is ambiguous, the editor has tried his best to preserve what seems to be the poet's intent.

On the surface, the *Sonnets* are arrayed into three main groups: the bulk of the first section (1-17) is thought to be addressed to a "fair youth"—a young man, most likely of noble birth**—in whom Shakespeare has taken a particular interest, whether for reasons of personal affinity or professional commission. The last section (127-154) deals largely with the "dark lady"—with whom the poet is apparently enamored, and whom the poet addresses in terms

---

*In fact, we may be presuming much by regarding the choices as coming from Shakespeare: given the uncertainty surrounding his participation in publishing the original Quarto of his sonnets, it is quite possible that the choice was that of the publisher, rather than the author.

Of course, authors have often blamed editors for stealing the soul from their writing. In the case of Shakespeare the accusation has obvious validity, even to the present day.

**Though entirely a matter of guess, speculation, and conjecture, it is quite likely that the "fair youth" was Henry Wriothesley, the young Earl of Southampton, who appears to have assisted the promising playwright after an outbreak of plague closed the theaters in the early 1590s. Another good possibility is William Herbert, Earl of Pembroke, who was also one of Shakespeare's patrons, and to whom the 1623 edition of Shakespeare's folio was dedicated.

suggesting passion or sexual obsession. The rest contain thoughts and sentiments that have fascinated scholars for centuries, often reflecting more about the era of the scholar than the mind of the poet. Still, though lost in the development of English in the last four centuries, most languages distinguish between second person singular and plural—the former denoting intimacy, the latter denoting deference or politeness. Therefore, in Shakespeare's day, the use of "thou" connoted a social inferior, or someone with whom the speaker shares a close personal relationship; "you" was used more formally. Given the strict class structure of English Society in Shakespeare's day, this may give us actual clues into the relationship between the poet and his various subjects—some of whom may have been patrons, friends, or lovers—as well as helping us sense his own view of the world he saw around him.

If viewed as addressed to the "fair youth," many of the sonnets contain images and sentiments that modern eyes would describe as markedly homoerotic. This has led, over the years, to much speculation about Shakespeare's sexual proclivities, which the absence of evidence has done nothing to curb. Even so, friendship among men in Shakespeare's day was less obsessed with homophobia, and affectionate sentiments among men were expressed more freely than in later years. Moreover, many of the sonnets give voice to a love without sexuality as well as a sexuality without love; this has led some to conclude that Shakespeare was giving voice to new, subjective ideas about human relationships—the notion that what is in the heart often lies hidden beneath convention—and struggling to find an appropriate language to express it.* In addition, the vast majority of the poems do not identify the subject's gender: only one-fifth of them are clearly addressed to one sex or the other, and many seem addressed to a sponsor or patron, who apparently also fancied and supported other poets of the day. The result is confusion on many counts, including the real objects of the poet's affection. And so, as one noted commentator has observed,

---

*See, eg, Kay, *Shakespeare*, pp 270-280.

Introduction

"William Shakespeare was almost certainly homosexual, bisexual, or heterosexual. The sonnets provide no evidence on the matter."*

As with the question of identity, in the end it matters very little: the sonnets convey intimate thoughts on love and friendship, from one of the greatest humanistic writers who ever walked the Earth. The rest is idle gossip—of the sort fit for those "that like of hearsay well."** Some scholars believe that his sonnets show the private Shakespeare, opening his heart to those closest to him. Others are convinced that they simply reflect the poet at play, entertaining his friends with his bawdy wit and facility with the English language. Each sonnet, however, will strike the reader in a different way; and in this sense, they are truly among his most private expressions.

The differences between the English language of today, and the language of Shakespeare's day stem more from idiom and common usage than vocabulary. Like most gifted writers, Shakespeare preferred the familiar to the esoteric, and while his vocabulary was immense, he used it to harness and channel the power of his words, and possessed an unmatched ear for a simple yet profound turn of phrase. We see this often in his plays, where many of his passages have become so commonplace we do not always recognize their origin: our "dogs of war,"*** and "winters of discontent"**** do not, after all, come with footnoted references in everyday speech, yet we recognize the power and majesty of the expressions. And though his sonnets contain fewer expressions that have become shorthand references for everyday life, the color and vividness of their imagery is no less profound. The "surley sullen bell" that the "churl death" may, on occasion, employ "time's injurious hand" to mark the "chronicle of wasted time" may evoke emotions just as sorrowful as

---

* Booth, ed. *Shakespeare's Sonnets, Edited with Analytic Commentary.* (1977), p 548.

** Sonnet 21.

*** *Julius Caesar*, 3.1.273.

**** *Richard III*, 1.1.1.

those in any of his plays—even as the "raiment of my heart" may lead to the joyful "marriage of true minds."* That they may be less familiar may simply suggest that the theater has enjoyed a wider audience over the years, and that people spend more time watching entertainment than quietly reading poetry.

While Shakespeare often sounds flowery and obscure to modern ears, his plays were quite popular in his day. While his use of language was elevated and often lofty, this reflected the loftiness of high artistic purpose, not intellectual snobbery. His plays were aimed squarely at where they would be most profitable—at the general public—and were attended by many who were not members of the intellectual elite of the day. His plays, like his verses, were understood and grasped by the masses as well as the upper crust. It is the difference in the common language of the day—Elizabethan English for Shakespeare, 21st Century Modern English for us—that today makes him seem obscure or unattainable. But just as we can easily understand the lesser poetry of our own stage, it is a mistake to suppose that Shakespeare was as mysterious and difficult to the playgoers of his age as he is to us. Oscar Hammerstein and Steven Sondheim are not, after all, beyond the comprehension of ordinary folk today; Shakespeare would have been just as accessible to his own audience, no matter what kinds of challenges he presents to us.

And yet once we understand those differences, Shakespeare opens up like a rose, revealing much about the human condition—the thorns as well as the sweetness. The notes that accompany the verses in this volume, while an inadequate attempt to "translate" the Elizabethan into the modern, are an effort to make his *Sonnets* more accessible to the modern reader. Unfortunately, many of the subtle nuances and interplays of words may be obscure to the modern reader, owing to the changes in common usage over the last four centuries. The formalized structure will present its own share of challenges—and the confusion caused by the occasional misfiring of our modern cerebral cortexes will only exacerbate the

---

*Sonnets 71, 32, 63, 106, 22, and 116, respectively.

other misunderstandings that the passage of time may present. But at least knowing what the poet was talking about will give the reader the chance to unlock some of the insights into the human soul that Shakespeare presents to the discerning reader. It is the editor's hope that this, in turn, will help the reader open some of the loveliest, tenderest, and most personal verses known to English literature.

Shakespeare's Sonnets

1

From fairest creatures we desire increase,
That thereby beauty's rose might never die,
But as the riper should by time decease,
His tender heir might bear his memory.
But thou, contracted to thine own bright eyes,
Feed'st thy light's flame with self-substantial fuel,
Making a famine where abundance lies,
Thyself thy foe, to thy sweet self too cruel.
Thou, that art now the world's fresh ornament
And only herald to the gaudy spring,
Within thine own bud buriest thy content
And, tender churl, makest waste in niggarding.
   Pity the world, or else this glutton be,
    To eat the world's due, by the grave and thee.

NOTES: As with many of the ensuing sonnets, this one reminds the subject of the briefness of Life. Here, the poet suggests that only by reproducing itself will beauty survive. **Line 1,** *increase*: reproduction. **Line 4,** *tender*: young; *bear his memory*: carry his image as a legacy. **Line 5,** *contracted to thy own bright eyes*: betrothed to your own image. As a play on words "contracted" also carries the meaning of "shrunken." **Line 6,** *self-substantial*: internally derived; from one's own substance. **Line 11,** *Within...thy content*: lose your posterity—*ie*, your child. **Line 12,** *churl*: miser (also, "boor" or "lowbrow"); *niggarding*: being miserly. **Line 14,** *To eat...and thee*: to deprive the world of your posterity.

2

When forty winters shall beseige thy brow,
And dig deep trenches in thy beauty's field,
Thy youth's proud livery, so gazed on now,
Will be a tattered weed, of small worth held.
Then, being asked where all thy beauty lies,
Where all the treasure of thy lusty days,
To say, within thine own deep-sunken eyes,
Were an all-eating shame and thriftless praise.
How much more praise deserved thy beauty's use,
If thou couldst answer: "This fair child of mine
Shall sum my count, and make my old excuse,"
Proving his beauty by succession thine!
   This were to be new made when thou art old,
   And see thy blood warm when thou feel'st it cold.

NOTES: Again noting the shortness of Time, the poet is posing alternative futures
to the subject: one in which the subject wastes the treasure of his youthful beauty;
the other in which he invests in his posterity by siring a child. **Lines 1-2,** *besiege thy
brow...dig deep trenches in thy beauty's field*: the image is one of a battle between youthful
beauty and the ravages of time, with Time laying siege (and digging trenches) in the
field of battle (ie, the subject's brow). **Line 3,** *proud livery*: magnificent clothing.
Line 6, *lusty*: strong and vigorous, with connotations of youthful lust. **Line 8,** *all-
eating*: consuming; *thriftless*: worthless. **Line 6,** *sum my count*: balance my accounts;
make my old excuse: excuse me for being old. **Line 12,** *Proving...by succession thine*:
showing that your child's beauty was an inheritance from you.

3

Look in thy glass, and tell the face thou viewest
Now is the time that face should form another,
Whose fresh repair, if now thou not renewest,
Thou dost beguile the world, unbless some mother.
For where is she so fair, whose uneared womb
Disdains the tillage of thy husbandry?
Or who is he so fond, will be the tomb
Of his self-love, to stop posterity?
Thou art thy mother's glass, and she in thee
Calls back the lovely April of her prime.
So thou, through windows of thine age shall see
Despite of wrinkles, this thy golden time.
   But if thou live, remembered not to be,
   Die single, and thine image dies with thee.

NOTES: The poet is reminding the subject that as he sees the reflection of his own beautiful mother when he looks in the mirror, so too the subject should someday see his own self reflected in his child. This verse also shows signs of Shakespeare's bawdy sense of humor. **Line 1,** *glass:* mirror (ie, looking glass). **Line 3,** *fresh repair:* youthful state. **Line 4,** *unbless some mother:* deprive some woman of the blessings of motherhood. **Line 5,** *uneared:* untilled or unplowed (Not the most romantic of Shakespeare's sexual images). **Line 6,** *tillage of thy husbandry:* (underscoring the "plowing" imagery of the previous line, and clarifying the sexual pun). **Lines 7-8,** *fond:* foolish; *be the tomb...to stop posterity:* bury the hope of future generations through his own narcissism. **Line 9,** *glass:* image or reflection. **Line 11:** *windows of thine age:* your eyes when you are old.

4

Unthrifty loveliness, why dost thou spend
Upon thyself thy beauty's legacy?
Nature's bequest gives nothing, but doth lend
And, being frank, she lends to those are free.
Then, beauteous niggard, why dost thou abuse
The bounteous largess given thee to give?
Profitless usurer, why dost thou use
So great a sum of sums, yet canst not live?
For, having traffic with thyself alone,
Thou of thyself thy sweet self dost deceive.
Then how, when nature calls thee to be gone,
What acceptable audit canst thou leave?
   Thy unused beauty must be tombed with thee,
   Which, usèd, lives th' executor to be.

NOTES: This sonnet continues the theme of beauty as treasure that should be invested wisely in future generations, **Line 1,** *Unthrifty*: profligate or selfish. **Line 2** *thy beauty's legacy*: inherited beauty. **Line 4,** *frank*: generous, liberal; *free*: generous. **Line 6,** *largess*: bounty. **Line 7,** *Profitless usurer*: moneylender who earns nothing with his treasure. **Line 8,** *live*: survive. **Line 9,** *having traffic with thyself alone*: doing business only with yourself. **Line 10,** *deceive*: cheat. **Line 14,** *executor*: the surviving heir or agent who carries on the estate of the deceased.

5

Those hours, that with gentle work did frame
The lovely gaze where every eye doth dwell,
Will play the tyrants to the very same,
And that unfair which fairly doth excel.
For never-resting time leads summer on
To hideous winter and confounds him there,
Sap checked with frost, and lusty leaves quite gone,
Beauty o'ersnowed, and bareness every where.
Then, were not summer's distillation left,
A liquid prisoner pent in walls of glass,
Beauty's effect with beauty were bereft,
Nor it, nor no remembrance what it was.
    But flowers distilled, though they with winter meet,
    Leese but their show; their substance still lives sweet.

NOTES: In this sonnet and the next one, the poet likens the subject to summer flowers that the coming winter will destroy, noting that the essence of the flowers can be preserved if distilled into perfume. **Line 1,** *frame*: make or form. **Line 2,** *gaze*: object viewed. **Line 4,** *unfair*: render ugly. **Line 6,** *confounds*: destroys. **Line 9,** *distillation*: perfume. **Line 10,** *liquid prisoner pent in walls of glass*: perfume in a bottle. (Shakespeare's image seems a more compelling way to put it). **Line 11,** *effect*: product; *with beauty were bereft*: were lost along with beauty. **Line 14,** *Leese*: lose; *substance*: essence. (The "essence" of the closing duplet is that flowers distilled into perfume lose only their outward appearance, while their enduring nature—ie, their sweet essence—lives on).

6

Then let not winter's ragged hand deface
In thee thy summer, ere thou be distilled.
Make sweet some vial; treasure thou some place
With beauty's treasure, ere it be self-killed.
That use is not forbidden usury
Which happies those that pay the willing loan.
That's for thyself to breed another thee,
Or ten times happier, be it ten for one.
Ten times thyself were happier than thou art,
If ten of thine ten times refigured thee.
Then what could death do, if thou shouldst depart,
Leaving thee living in posterity?
  Be not self-willed, for thou art much too fair
  To be death's conquest, and make worms thine heir.

NOTES: This poem follows the theme from the previous sonnet, the poet noting that children would make the subject immortal. **Line 3,** *vial*: a vessel for holding the perfume distilled in the previous sonnet (the sexual connotation is probably intentional); *treasure*: enrich. **Line 5,** *usury*: the lending of money at high rates of interest, which Elizabethans regarded as "un-Christian." **Lines 5-6,** *That use is not forbidden usury which happies those that pay the willing loan*: that which elates those who gladly repay the debt is not usury. **Line 10,** *refigured*: duplicated, reproduced. **Line 13,** *self-willed*: selfishly stubborn, or bequeathing to yourself.

7

Lo! in the orient, when the gracious light
Lifts up his burning head, each undereye
Doth homage to his new-appearing sight,
Serving with looks his sacred majesty.
And, having climbed the steep-up heavenly hill,
Resembling strong youth in his middle age,
Yet mortal looks adore his beauty still,
Attending on his golden pilgrimage.
But when from high-most pitch, with weary car,
Like feeble age he reeleth from the day,
The eyes, 'fore duteous, now converted are
From his low tract, and look another way.
    So thou, thyself outgoing in thy noon,
    Unlooked on diest, unless thou get a son.

NOTES: This sonnet likens the path of the sun in the sky to the path of a mortal man. **Line 1**, *the gracious light*: the sun. **Line 2**, *undereye*: eye of those on earth. **Line 8**, *Attending on*: serving; waiting upon. **Line 9**, *highmost pitch*: zenith; high point; *car*: carriage or chariot. **Line 11**, *'fore*: before; *converted are*: are turned. **Line 12**, *tract*: path. **Line 13**: *outgoing in thy noon*: beginning to decline even at the pinnacle of life. **Line 14**, *get*: beget.

8

Music to hear, why hear'st thou music sadly?
Sweets with sweets war not, joy delights in joy.
Why lov'st thou that which thou receiv'st not gladly,
Or else receiv'st with pleasure thine annoy?
If the true concord of well-tunèd sounds
By unions married do offend thine ear,
They do but sweetly chide thee, who confounds
In singleness the parts that thou shouldst bear.
Mark how one string, sweet husband to another,
Strikes each in each by mutual ordering,
Resembling sire and child and happy mother,
Who, all in one, one pleasing note do sing—
   Whose speechless song, being many, seeming one,
   Sings this to thee: "Thou single wilt prove none."

NOTES: The poet again chides the subject for declining to engage in the sweet harmonies of "sire and child and happy mother," suggesting that the reason he seems to take little pleasure in music is that its harmonies remind him that he is not making procreative music himself. **Line 1,** *music to hear*: you who are like music to the ear. **Line 3,** *Why lov'st thou*: why do you bother with. **Line 4,** *receiv'st with pleasure thine annoy*: enjoy being displeased. **Line 6,** *unions married:* combinations. **Lines 9-12,** *Mark how one string...one pleasing note do sing*: Note how the strings of an instrument, struck together, produce one pleasing harmony. **Lines 13-14:** *Whose speechless song...single wilt prove none*: the instrument shows that a single string produces no music.

9

Is it for fear to wet a widow's eye
That thou consumest thyself in single life?
Ah! if thou issueless shalt hap to die
The world will wail thee, like a makeless wife.
The world will be thy widow, and still weep
That thou no form of thee hast left behind,
When every private widow well may keep
By children's eyes her husband's shape in mind.
Look, what an unthrift in the world doth spend
Shifts but his place, for still the world enjoys it;
But beauty's waste hath in the world an end,
And, kept unused, the user so destroys it.
   No love toward others in that bosom sits
   That, on himself, such murderous shame commits.

NOTES: The poet observes that if the reason the subject is reluctant to marry is because he does not wish to leave behind a grieving widow, he will instead leave behind a world grieving that his beauty has no heir. **Line 3,** *issueless*: without heirs, childless; *hap*: happen. **Line 4,** *wail*: mourn; *makeless*: mateless; widowed. **Line 5,** *still*: always, ever. **Line 6,** *form*: image. **Line 10-11,** *Look what an unthrift...the world enjoys it*: ie, the money a wastrel spends is widely spread so that everyone can benefit. **Line 12,** *unused, user*: "use" is often employed in the service of Shakespeare's many sexual puns. This line conveys the hint that wasting the subject's beauty by failing to employ it for sexual adventures will result in its destruction.

10

For shame, deny that thou bear'st love to any
Who for thyself art so unprovident.
Grant, if thou wilt, thou art beloved of many,
But that thou none lov'st is most evident.
For thou art so possessed with murderous hate
That 'gainst thyself thou stick'st not to conspire,
Seeking that beauteous roof to ruinate
Which to repair should be thy chief desire.
O, change thy thought, that I may change my mind!
Shall hate be fairer lodged than gentle love?
Be, as thy presence is, gracious and kind,
Or to thyself, at least, kind-hearted prove.
　　Make thee another self, for love of me,
　　That beauty still may live in thine or thee.

NOTES: Continuing the "murderous" imagery that closes the previous sonnet, the poet suggests that the subject's unwillingness to mate is the result of self-hatred. **Line 2,** *unprovident*: improvident. **Line 6,** *stick'st not*: are willing; do not hesitate. **Line 7,** *roof*: family, lineage; *ruinate*: destroy. **Line 9,** *change thy thought*: change your way of thinking. **Line 11,** *presence*: outward appearance.

11

As fast as thou shalt wane, so fast thou grow'st
In one of thine, from that which thou departest;
And that fresh blood which youngly thou bestowest
Thou mayst call thine, when thou from youth covertest.
Herein lives wisdom, beauty and increase;
Without this, folly, age and cold decay.
If all were minded so, the times should cease,
And threescore year would make the world away.
Let those whom nature hath not made for store,
Harsh, featureless, and rude, barrenly perish;
Look, whom she best endowed she gave the more,
Which bounteous gift thou shouldst in bounty cherish.
   She carved thee for her seal, and meant thereby
   Thou shouldst print more, not let that copy die.

NOTES: The poet again reminds the subject that the vitality of Life is renewed by reproduction, and suggests that Nature intended him to have children. **Lines 1-2,** *As fast as...which thou departest*: As you begin to age, your child would be approaching the very prime that you are leaving. **Line 3,** *youngly*: in youth. **Line 4,** *convertest*: depart. **Lines 7-8,** *If all were minded...the world away*. If everyone remained childless, then Mankind would perish after a single generation. **Line 9,** *for store*: ie, for breeding. **Line 12,** *cherish*: safeguard, protect. **Line 13,** *seal*: ie, a seal which was used to make an impression in wax. (Not the aquatic kind).

12

When I do count the clock that tells the time,
And see the brave day sunk in hideous night;
When I behold the violet past prime,
And sable curls all silvered o'er with white;
When lofty trees I see barren of leaves,
Which erst from heat did canopy the herd,
And summer's green all girded up in sheaves
Borne on the bier with white and bristly beard;
Then, of thy beauty do I question make,
That thou among the wastes of time must go,
Since sweets and beauties do themselves forsake
And die as fast as they see others grow;
    And nothing 'gainst time's scythe can make defense
    Save breed, to brave him when he takes thee hence.

NOTES: This verse employs the symbolism of relentless Time—from clock, to seasons, to the final harvest. **Line 1,** *count the clock*: ie, the time sounded on a clock tower. **Line 2,** *brave*: glorious. **Line 4,** *sable*: black. **Line 6,** *erst*: in the recent past. **Lines 7-8,** *And summer's green...white and bristly beard*: The summer's crops, now harvested. **Line 9,** *do question make*: wonder about; ponder. **Line 14,** *breed*: offspring; *brave*: defy.

13

O, that you were yourself! But, love, you are
No longer yours than you yourself here live.
Against this coming end you should prepare,
And your sweet semblance to some other give.
So should that beauty, which you hold in lease,
Find no determination, then you were
Yourself again after yourself's decease,
When your sweet issue your sweet form should bear.
Who lets so fair a house fall to decay,
Which husbandry in honor might uphold
Against the stormy gusts of winter's day
And barren rage of death's eternal cold?
   O, none but unthrifts! Dear my love, you know
   You had a father; let your son say so.

NOTES: In his verse, the poet is likening the subject to a spendthrift, who lets his house fall into decay before the coming winter. **Line 3,** *this coming end:* ie, death. **Line 5,** *hold in lease:* ie, have temporarily, possess for the moment. **Line 6,** *determination:* ending (ie, an end to the lease). **Line 10,** *husbandry:* proper management (and using "husband" as a pun, suggesting the need to marry). **Line 13,** *unthrifts:* spendthrifts.

14

Not from the stars do I my judgment pluck,
And yet methinks I have astronomy,
But not to tell of good or evil luck,
Of plagues, of dearths, or seasons' quality.
Nor can I fortune to brief minutes tell,
Pointing to each his thunder, rain, and wind;
Or say with princes if it shall go well
By oft predict that I in heaven find.
But from thine eyes my knowledge I derive,
And constant stars, in them I read such art
As truth and beauty shall together thrive
If from thyself to store thou wouldst convert.
    Or else of thee this I prognosticate:
    Thy end is truth's and beauty's doom and date.

NOTES: One of many sonnets employing the image of astrology, here the poet is taking his astrological readings from the "constant stars" of the subject's eyes. **Line 1:** *my judgment pluck*: draw my conclusions. **Line 2,** *astronomy*: astrology. **Line 8,** *oft predict*: frequent astrological signs. **Line 12,** *If from thyself...wouldst convert*: If you would start thinking about having children instead of thinking only of yourself. **Line 14,** *Thy end...doom and date*: You death will be doomsday for beauty and truth.

15

When I consider every thing that grows
Holds in perfection but a little moment,
That this huge stage presenteth nought but shows
Whereon the stars in secret influence commént;
When I perceive that men as plants increase,
Cheerèd and checked even by the self-same sky,
Vaunt in their youthful sap, at height decrease,
And wear their brave state out of memory;
Then, the conceit of this inconstant stay
Sets you most rich in youth before my sight,
Where wasteful time debateth with decay
To change your day of youth to sullied night.
   And all in war with Time for love of you,
   As he takes from you, I engraft you new.

NOTES: This verse, like many others, suggests that the writer's poetry may bestow immortality on the subject. **Line 3,** *shows*: entertainments. **Line 4,** *secret influence commént*: wield hidden power. **Line 5,** *increase*: thrive. **Line 6,** *cheerèd and checked*: applauded and booed; or encouraged and restrained. **Line 7,** *Vaunt*: rejoice or celebrate. **Line 9,** *conceit*: thought or idea; *inconstant stay*: changing condition. **Line 11,** *debateth*: contends with. **Line 12,** *sullied*: darkened. **Line 14:** *engraft*: ie, place or graft you into my poem (continuing the plant imagery that precedes it).

16

But wherefore do not you a mightier way
Make war upon this bloody tyrant, Time?
And fortify yourself in your decay
With means more blessèd than my barren rhyme?
Now stand you on the top of happy hours,
And many maiden gardens yet unset,
With virtuous wish would bear your living flowers,
Much liker than your painted counterfeit.
So should the lines of life that life repair
Which this time's pencil, or my pupil pen,
Neither in inward worth nor outward fair
Can make you live yourself in eyes of men.
   To give away yourself keeps yourself still,
     And you must live, drawn by your own sweet skill.

NOTES: Following the theme of the previous sonnet, this verse suggests that procreation might be both a "mightier" and "more blessèd" way to immortality than poetry. **Line 1,** *wherefore*: why. **Line 6,** *unset*: unplanted (Planting flowers in the maiden gardens was probably the "more blessèd" way to immortality the poet had in mind; it also continues the "plant" imagery from the preceding sonnet). **Line 7,** *with virtuous wish*: with hopes of marriage. **Line 8,** *liker than your painted counterfeit*: more like you than your mere image or portrait. **Line 9,** *lines of life*: descendants. **Line 10,** *Time's pencil*: today's artists; *pupil pen*: beginner's writings. **Line 11:** *fair*: beauty. **Line 13,** *give away yourself*: ie, marry.

17

Who will believe my verse in time to come
If it were filled with your most high deserts?
Though yet, Heaven knows, it is but as a tomb
Which hides your life and shows not half your parts.
If I could write the beauty of your eyes,
And in fresh numbers all your graces,
The age to come would say, "This poet lies!
Such heavenly touches ne'er touched earthly faces."
So should my papers, yellowed with their age,
Be scorned, like old men of less truth than tongue,
And your true rights be termed a poet's rage,
And stretchèd meter of an antique song.
  But were some child of yours alive that time,
  You should live twice, in it and in my rhyme.

NOTES: The poet is complaining that without proof everyone will think his poetic tributes to the subject are all artistic nonsense, and advises the subject that children convey a second (and presumably more trustworthy) way to immortality **Line 2,** *most high deserts*: very best qualities. **Line 4,** *parts*: best qualities. **Line 6,** *fresh numbers*: new verses; *charms*: charms. **Line 11,** *true rights*: the acclaim which is due you; *a poet's rage*: poetic license. **Line 12:** *stretchèd meter*: poor or exaggerated poetry.

18

Shall I compare thee to a summer's day?
Thou art more lovely and more temperate.
Rough winds do shake the darling buds of May,
And summer's lease hath all too short a date.
Sometime too hot the eye of heaven shines,
And often is his gold complexion dimmed.
And every fair from fair sometime declines,
By chance or nature's changing course untrimmed.
But thy eternal summer shall not fade
Nor lose possession of that fair thou ow'st;
Nor shall death brag thou wander'st in his shade
When in eternal lines to time thou growest.
  So long as men can breathe or eyes can see,
  So long lives this, and this gives life to thee.

NOTES: One of Shakespeare's best known sonnets, this verse notes that the subject is milder and prettier than the loveliest day...before returning to the theme of immortality through poetry. **Line 2,** *temperate*: mild—both of temperature and disposition. **Line 4:** *summer's lease hath all too short a date*: summer passes all too quickly. (A lease is a temporary legal entitlement, which expires at a set time). **Line 5,** *the eye of heaven*: ie, the sun. **Line 7,** *every fair from fair sometime declines*: all things of beauty eventually come to an end. **Line 8,** *untrimmed*: deprived of beauty. **Line 10,** *that fair thou ow'st*: the beauty you possess. **Line 12:** *eternal lines*: immortal poetry. **Line 14:** *this*: ie, this verse.

19

Devouring Time, blunt thou the lion's paws,
And make the earth devour her own sweet brood.
Pluck the keen teeth from the fierce tiger's jaws,
And burn the long-lived phoenix in her blood.
Make glad and sorry seasons as thou fleet'st,
And do whate'er thou wilt, swift-footed time,
To the wide world and all her fading sweets.
But I forbid thee one most heinous crime:
O, carve not with thy hours my love's fair brow,
Nor draw no lines there with thine antique pen.
Him in thy course untainted do allow,
For beauty's pattern to succeeding men.
   Yet, do thy worst, old time: despite thy wrong,
   My love shall in my verse ever live young.

NOTES: Drawing upon several Latin proverbs, this verse calls upon Time not to work its destruction upon the subject. **Line 1,** *Devouring Time*: this recalls Ovid's line that "Time devours all things ("*tempus edax rerums*"). **Line 4,** *phoenix*: the mythical creature that is reborn from its own ashes. **Line 5,** *fleet'st*: pass quickly. **Line 6,** *swift-footed time*: from *tempus fugit* (continuing the motif of Latin proverbs). **Line 7,** *sweets*: delights.

20

A woman's face with Nature's own hand painted
Hast thou, the master mistress of my passion;
A woman's gentle heart, but not acquainted
With shifting change, as is false women's fashion;
An eye more bright than theirs, less false in rolling,
Gilding the object whereupon it gazeth;
A man in hue, all hues in his controlling,
Much steals men's eyes and women's souls amazeth.
And for a woman wert thou first created,
Till Nature, as she wrought thee, fell a-doting,
And by addition me of thee defeated,
By adding one thing to my purpose nothing.
    But since she pricked thee out for women's pleasure,
    Mine be thy love, and thy love's use their treasure.

NOTES: Addressed to the "fair youth," the poet speculates that Nature started out to create a beautiful woman but, falling in love with her creation, changed the subject to a man instead. The poem is also unusual for its use of "feminine" rhymes. **Line 6,** *Gilding*: illuminating; or turning to gold. **Line 7,** *A man...his controlling*. Some academics are convinced that there is a pun hidden here, but are unable to discern its meaning. The "hue" may simply be a play on the word "who." Or, the "fair youth" of the sonnets may, as Oscar Wilde claimed, be a young actor named "Hughes." See, Harrison, *Shakespeare: The Complete Works,* (1948) p 1594. **Line 9,** *for*: as. **Lines 11-12,** *by addition...to my purpose nothing*: cheated me out of you by adding something (ie, a penis) of no use to me. **Line 13,** *pricked*: picked (as well as a vulgar pun). **Line 14,** *use*: another of Shakespeare's bawdy puns, "use" is employed here to connote sexual enjoyment, as well as the more prosaic sense of profit or employment.

21

So is it not with me as with that Muse
Stirred by a painted beauty to his verse,
Who heaven itself for ornament doth use,
And every fair with his fair doth rehearse,
Making a couplement of proud compare
With sun and moon, with earth and sea's rich gems,
With April's first-born flowers, and all things rare
That heaven's air in this huge rondure hems.
O, let me, true in love, but truly write,
And then believe me—my love is as fair
As any mother's child, though not so bright
As those gold candles fixed in heaven's air.
  Let them say more that like of hearsay well.
  I will not praise that purpose not to sell.

NOTES: The poet contrasts his approach—that of simply telling the truth about the one he loves—with those other poets who exaggerate their loves by making grand comparisons. **Line 1,** *Muse*: poet. **Line 2,** *painted beauty*: ie, one whose beauty is artificial (ie, needs to be painted on, rather than coming naturally). **Line 3,** *heaven itself...doth use*: uses comparisons with heaven. **Line 4,** *And every fair...doth rehearse*: And compares every beautiful thing to his beloved. **Line 5,** *Making a couplement...compare*: Joining together, for the purposes of comparison. **Line 7,** *all things rare*: everything splendid or outstanding. **Line 8:** *rondure*: the earth. **Line 12,** *gold candles fixed in heaven's air*: the stars in the sky. **Line 13,** *like of hearsay well*: enjoy gossip or rumors. **Line 14,** *I will not...not to sell*: My compliments are not for my own selfish reasons.

22

My glass shall not persuade me I am old
So long as youth and thou are of one date.
But when in thee time's furrows I behold,
Then look I death my days should expiate.
For all that beauty that doth cover thee
Is but the seemly raiment of my heart,
Which in thy breast doth live, as thine in me:
How can I then be elder than thou art?
O therefore, love, be of thyself so wary
As I, not for myself, but for thee will,
Bearing thy heart, which I will keep so chary
As tender nurse her babe from faring ill.
   Presume not on thy heart when mine is slain;
   Thou gav'st me thine, not to give back again.

NOTES: Here, the poet expounds on the idea of love as an exchange of hearts. **Line 1,** *glass*: mirror. **Line 2,** *are of one date*: are the same age. **Line 4,** *look I*: I will expect; *expiate*: come to an end. **Line 6,** *seemly raiment*: beautiful clothing. **Line 11,** *chary*: carefully, tenderly. **Line 13,** *Presume not on*: do not expect to reclaim.

23

As an unperfect actor on the stage,
Who with his fear is put besides his part,
Or some fierce thing replete with too much rage,
Whose strength's abundance weakens his own heart,
So I, for fear of trust, forget to say
The perfect ceremony of love's rite,
And in mine own love's strength seem to decay,
O'ercharged with burden of mine own love's might.
O, let my books be then the eloquence
And dumb presagers of my speaking breast,
Who plead for love and look for recompense
More than that tongue that more hath more expressed.
  O, learn to read what silent love hath writ;
  To hear with eyes belongs to love's fine wit.

NOTES: Blaming his inability to speak of love to a lack of self-confidence, the poet asks that the subject be content with his written expressions. **Line 1,** *unperfect*: imperfect. **Line 2,** *Who with his fear is put besides his part*: who, being afraid, forgets his lines. **Line 4,** *strength's abundance*: excessive power. **Line 5-6,** *I, for fear...love's rite*: being shy, I fail to demonstrate my love outwardly. **Line 9,** *books*: writings. **Line 10,** *dumb presagers*: mimes; *speaking breast*: what my heart would say. **Line 12,** *more hath more expressed*: that has usually had more to say. **Line 14,** *wit*: intelligence.

24

Mine eye hath played the painter, and hath stelled
Thy beauty's form in table of my heart.
My body is the frame wherein 'tis held,
And pérspective it is best painter's art.
For through the painter must you see his skill,
To find where your true image pictured lies,
Which in my bosom's shop is hanging still,
That hath his windows glazèd with thine eyes.
Now see what good turns eyes for eyes have done:
Mine eyes have drawn thy shape, and thine for me
Are windows to my breast, wherethrough the sun
Delights to peep, to gaze therein on thee.
   Yet eyes this cunning want to grace their art;
   They draw but what they see, know not the heart.

NOTES: This verse casts the poet as capturing the image of the beloved like a painting in his own heart. **Line 1,** *stelled*: captured, fixed. **Line 2,** *table*: canvas; the surface of a painting. **Line 7,** *shop*: ie, the artists workshop. **Line 8,** *That hath his windows glazèd with thine eyes*: that uses your eyes to provide the glass fitted for the shop's windows. **Line 11,** *wherethrough*: through which. **Line 13,** *want to grace*: lack the skill to adorn.

25

Let those who are in favor with their stars
Of public honor and proud titles boast,
Whilst I, whom fortune of such triumph bars,
Unlooked for joy in that I honor most.
Great princes' favorites their fair leaves spread,
But as the marigold at the sun's eye,
And in themselves their pride lies burièd,
For at a frown they in their glory die.
The painful warrior, famousèd for fight,
After a thousand victories once foiled
Is from the book of honor razèd quite,
And all the rest forgot for which he toiled.
   Then happy I, that love and am beloved
   Where I may not remove nor be removed.

NOTES: Contrasting his own state with those who appear to have everything in life—such as fame and power—the poet notes that their good fortune is subject to the whims of fortune, while he is content to know that his love will never change. **Line 1,** *in favor with their stars*: lucky. **Line 4,** *Unlooked for joy*: rejoice unnoticed. **Lines 5-6,** *Great princes'...at the sun's eye*: the reference is to public favorites who blossom only in the light of attention. **Line 9,** *painful*: struggling; *famousèd*: celebrated. Line 11, *razèd quite*: completely obliterated. **Line 14,** *remove nor be removed*: leave or be forced to leave.

26

Lord of my love, to whom in vassalage
Thy merit hath my duty strongly knit,
To thee I send this written embassage
To witness duty, not to show my wit.
Duty so great, which wit so poor as mine
May make seem bare, in wanting words to show it,
But that I hope some good conceit of thine
In thy soul's thought, all naked, will bestow it;
Till whatsoever star that guides my moving
Points on me graciously with fair aspéct,
And puts apparel on my tattered loving
To show me worthy of thy sweet respect.
   Then may I dare to boast how I do love thee;
   Till then not show my head where thou mayst prove me.

NOTES: Likening his love to the allegiance due to a feudal lord, the poet bestows his insignificant verse as an offering of duty, hoping someday to be worthy of similar devotion in return. **Line 1,** *vassalage*: the devotion of a loyal servant. **Line 2,** *duty*: "duty" is used to connote homage or respect, as well as the duty a vassal owes to the lord. **Line 3,** *embassage*: communiqué or message. **Line 4,** *witness duty*: to demonstrate devotion. **Line 6,** *bare*: paltry or insignificant; *wanting words to show it*: lacking the words to express it. **Line 7,** *conceit*: thought or opinion. **Lines 9-10,** *whatsoever star...with fair aspéct*: whichever star controls my life shines favorably upon me. **Line 14,** *prove*: test.

27

Weary with toil, I haste me to my bed,
The dear repose for limbs with travel tired,
But then begins a journey in my head
To work my mind, when body's work's expired.
For then my thoughts, from far where I abide,
Intend a zealous pilgrimage to thee,
And keep my drooping eyelids open wide,
Looking on darkness which the blind do see.
Save that my soul's imaginary sight
Presents thy shadow to my sightless view,
Which, like a jewel hung in ghastly night,
Makes black night beauteous, and her old face new.
  Lo! thus, by day my limbs, by night my mind,
  For thee and for myself no quiet find.

NOTES: The poet laments the fact that thoughts of his beloved keep him from resting at night. **Line 2,** *limbs with travel tired*: a body weary from the day's exertions. **Line 6,** *Intend*: aim or direct. **Line 10,** *shadow*: image.

28

How can I then return in happy plight,
That I am debarred the benefit of rest?
When day's oppression is not eased by night,
But day by night, and night by day, oppressed?
And each, though enemies to either's reign,
Do in consent shake hands to torture me,
The one by toil, the other to complain
How far I toil, still farther off from thee.
I tell the day, to please him, thou art bright,
And dost him grace when clouds do blot the heaven.
So flatter I the swart-complexioned night,
When sparkling stars twire not thou, gild'st the even.
  But day doth daily draw my sorrows longer;
   And night doth nightly make grief's length seem stronger.

NOTES: Developing the idea of nocturnal restlessness in the previous sonnet, the poet complains that night and day are conspiring to torture him—exhausting him by day; tormenting him with thoughts of his beloved by night. **Line 1,** *plight*: condition. **Line 2,** *debarred*: deprived of. **Line 11,** *swart*: dark; black. **Line 12,** *twire*: twinkle; *even*: evening.

29

When, in disgrace with fortune and men's eyes,
I all alone beweep my outcast state
And trouble deaf heaven with my bootless cries,
And look upon myself and curse my fate,
Wishing me like to one more rich in hope,
Featured like him, like him with friends possessed,
Desiring this man's art and that man's scope,
With what I most enjoy contented least;
Yet in these thoughts, myself almost despising,
Haply I think on thee, and then my state,
Like to the lark at break of day arising
From sullen earth, sings hymns at heaven's gate.
  For thy sweet love remembered such wealth brings
  That then I scorn to change my state with kings.

NOTES: Though saddened by his lowly station, the poet's spirits are raised by the subject's affections. **Line 2,** *beweep*: morn, cry over. **Line 3,** *bootless*: unavailing. **Line 6,** *Featured like*: looking like. **Line 10,** *Haply:* perhaps.

30

When to the sessions of sweet silent thought
I summon up remembrance of things past,
I sigh the lack of many a thing I sought,
And with old woes new wail my dear time's waste.
Then can I drown an eye, unused to flow,
For precious friends hid in death's dateless night,
And weep afresh love's long since cancelled woe,
And moan the expense of many a vanished sight.
Then can I grieve at grievances foregone,
And heavily from woe to woe tell o'er
The sad account of fore-bemoanèd moan,
Which I new pay, as if not paid before.
   But if the while I think on thee, dear friend,
   All losses are restored and sorrows end.

NOTES: Thinking of past disappointments and losses causes the poet new grief, thinking about his friendship with the subject always puts an end to his self-pity. **Line 1,** *sessions:* the reference is to the formal sittings of a court. **Line 4,** *with old woes...dear time's waste:* cry over past losses and wasted time all over again. **Line 5,** *drown an eye:* cry, or mourn. **Line 6,** *dateless:* eternal. **Line 8,** *expense:* waste. **Line 9,** *foregone:* already past.

31

Thy bosom is endearèd with all hearts
Which I by lacking have supposèd dead.
And there reigns love, and all love's loving parts,
And all those friends which I thought burièd.
How many a holy and obsequious tear
Hath dear religious love stol'n from mine eye
As interest of the dead, which now appear
But things removed that hidden in thee lie!
Thou art the grave where buried love doth live,
Hung with the trophies of my lovers gone,
Who all their parts of me to thee did give;
That due of many now is thine alone.
   Their images I loved I view in thee,
    And thou, all they, hast all the all of me.

NOTES: Using the imagery of death, the poet remembers many friends lost to time, but sees the renewal of his affections in the subject's person. **Line 1,** *is endeared with*: is made all the more precious by. **Line 5,** *obsequious*: mourning. **Line 6,** *religious*: pious. **Line 7,** *interest*: tribute. **Line 9,** *doth live*: survives. **Line 10,** *trophies*: memorials; *lovers*: dearest friends. (Lines 9-10 suggest the image of a mausoleum). **Line 11,** *their parts*: their share. **Line 12,** *that due of*: that owed to.

32

If thou survive my well-contented day,
When that churl Death my bones with dust shall cover,
And shalt by fortune once more resurvey
These poor rude lines of thy deceasèd lover,
Compare them with the bettering of the time,
And, though they be outstripped by every pen,
Reserve them for my love, not for their rhyme,
Exceeded by the height of happier men.
O, then vouchsafe me but this loving thought:
"Had my friend's Muse grown with this growing age,
A dearer birth than this his love had brought
To march in ranks of better equipage.
   But since he died and poets better prove,
   Theirs for their style I'll read, his for his love."

NOTES: The poet asks the subject to look past the meager poetry contained in his verses after the poet is gone and buried, and to savor the sentiments and affection expressed in them. **Line 1,** *well-contented*: happy. **Line 2,** *churl*: boor. **Line 3,** *by fortune*: by chance, perhaps; *resurvey*: look at again. **Line 5,** *bettering of the time*: ie, the better-written poems of the day. **Line 7,** *Reserve*: keep or hold on to. **Line 8,** *happier*: better. **Line 10,** *grown with this growing age*: arisen at a better time (ie, had the poet lived at a time of superior literary style). **Line 11,** *dearer birth*: worthier offspring. **Line 13,** *since he died...better prove*: since the poetry has gotten better since he died. (Not, however, implying any causal relationship between the two developments).

33

Full many a glorious morning have I seen
Flatter the mountain tops with sovereign eye,
Kissing with golden face the meadows green,
Gilding pale streams with heavenly alchemy,
Anon permit the basest clouds to ride
With ugly rack on his celestial face
And, from the forlorn world his visage hide,
Stealing unseen to west with this disgrace.
Even so, my sun one early morn did shine
With all triumphant splendor on my brow;
But out, alack! he was but one hour mine;
The region cloud hath masked him from me now.
   Yet him, for this, my love no whit disdaineth.
   Suns of the world may stain when heaven's sun staineth.

NOTES: In this verse, and the two sonnets following, the poet is chiding the subject for some perceived hurt. Here, the poet remarks that as even the sun can be obscured by clouds, people can sometimes hide their essential goodness behind clouds of their own. **Line 2,** *sovereign*: glorious, supreme.; *sovereign eye*: ie, the sun. **Line 4,** *Gilding*: lining with gold; *alchemy*: ie, the creation of gold from baser metals. **Line 6,** *rack*: a mass of clouds in the sky. **Line 12,** *region*: sky-inhabiting; heavenly. Line 14: *Suns of the world*: ie, people (a wordplay on suns-sons); *stain*: fade or become discolored (with overtones of moral corruption); *when heaven's sun staineth*: when the sun dims.

34

Why didst thou promise such a beauteous day,
And make me travel forth without my cloak,
To let base clouds o'ertake me in my way,
Hiding thy bravery in their rotten smoke?
'Tis not enough that through the cloud thou break
To dry the rain on my storm-beaten face,
For no man well of such a salve can speak
That heals the wound, and cures not the disgrace.
Nor can thy shame give physic to my grief;
Though thou repent, yet I have still the loss.
The offender's sorrow lends but weak relief
To him that bears the strong offense's cross.
   Ah! but those tears are pearl which thy love sheds,
   And they are rich and ransom all ill deeds.

NOTES: Continuing the theme from the previous verse, the poet accuses the subject of betraying him, much like a bright sun may deceive a traveler to go out without a cloak only to see the day turn rainy. The poet then remarks that the subject's tears of repentance are enough to atone for any damage done. **Line 1,** *thou*: the poem is addressed to the Sun. **Line 3,** *base*: dark. **Line 4,** *bravery*: splendor, glory; *smoke*: mist or fog. **Line 7,** *salve*: balm; healing ointment. **Line 8,** *disgrace*: dishonor. (The line suggests the proverb that "though the wound be healed, yet the scar remains"). **Line 9,** *give physic to*: cure or heal. **Lines 12-14,** *The offender's sorrow... offense's cross*: Apologies do not make the burden any less for those who must suffer the consequences.

35

No more be grieved at that which thou hast done.
Roses have thorns, and silver fountains mud;
Clouds and eclipses stain both moon and sun,
And loathsome canker lives in sweetest bud.
All men make faults, and even I in this,
Authorizing thy trespass with compare,
Myself corrupting, salving thy amiss,
Excusing thy sins more than thy sins are.
For to thy sensual fault I bring in sense—
Thy adverse party is thy advocate—
And 'gainst myself a lawful plea commence.
Such civil war is in my love and hate,
    That I an accessory needs must be
    To that sweet thief which sourly robs from me.

NOTES: The poet seeks to reassure the subject by noting that many lovely things are imperfect, only to accuse himself of complicity by finding excuses for the misbehavior. **Line 3,** *stain*: darken. **Line 4,** *canker*: ie, a cankerworm. **Line 5,** *make faults*: do wrong. **Line 6,** *Authorizing thy trespass with compare*: Excusing your offenses with my similes. **Line 7,** *Myself corrupting, salving thy amiss*: Abasing myself by excusing your faults. **Line 9,** *sense*: reason. **Line 10,** *advocate*: attorney. **Lines 10-14,** *adverse party is thy advocate...sourly robs from me*: the sequence applies the imagery of litigation in court, the poet noting that the offended party is acting as the subjects most forceful defender, as well as an accomplice to the misdeeds.

36

Let me confess that we two must be twain,
Although our undivided loves are one.
So shall those blots that do with me remain
Without thy help, by me be borne alone.
In our two loves there is but one respect,
Though in our lives a separable spite
Which, though it alter not love's sole effect,
Yet doth it steal sweet hours from love's delight.
I may not evermore acknowledge thee,
Lest my bewailèd guilt should do thee shame,
Nor thou with public kindness honor me,
Unless thou take that honor from thy name.
  But do not so; I love thee in such sort
  As, thou being mine, mine is thy good report.

NOTES: The poet is lamenting the fact that for the sake of the subject's honor, their love can never be acknowledged. **Line 1,** *confess:* admit. **Line 3,** *blots:* imperfections. **Line 4,** *borne:* suffered or endured. **Line 5,** *respect:* consideration. **Line 6,** *separable spite:* painful separation. **Line 7,** *effect:* result or outcome. **Line 9,** *evermore acknowledge:* publicly recognize our close relationship ever in the future. **Line 12:** *take that honor from thy name:* dishonor yourself. **Line 14,** *mine is thy good report:* I find satisfaction in your own good reputation.

37

As a decrepit father takes delight
To see his active child do deeds of youth,
So I, made lame by fortune's dearest spite,
Take all my comfort of thy worth and truth.
For whether beauty, birth, or wealth, or wit,
Or any of these all, or all, or more,
Entitled in thy parts do crownèd sit,
I make my love engrafted to this store.
So then, I am not lame, poor, nor despised,
Whilst that this shadow doth such substance give
That I, in thy abundance, am sufficed,
And by a part of all thy glory live.
    Look what is best, that best I wish in thee.
    This wish I have; then, ten times happy me!

NOTES: Laid low by cruel fortune, the poet nevertheless feels heartened that the same fortune has showered the subject with abundance. **Line 3,** *dearest*: cruelest, bitterest. **Line 4,** *of*: from. **Line 7,** *Entitled*: By right. **Line 8,** *engrafted*: joined; *store*: abundance. **Line 10,** *shadow*: hint, trace. **Line 13,** *Look what*: whatever.

38

How can my Muse want subject to invent
While thou dost breathe, that pour'st into my verse
Thine own sweet argument, too excellent
For every vulgar paper to rehearse?
O, give thyself the thanks, if aught in me
Worthy perusal stand against thy sight,
For who's so dumb that cannot write to thee,
When thou thyself dost give invention light?
Be thou the tenth Muse, ten times more in worth
Than those old nine which rhymers invocate;
And he that calls on thee, let him bring forth
Eternal numbers to outlive long date.
  If my slight Muse do please these curious days,
  The pain be mine, but thine shall be the praise.

NOTES: Here, the poet credits the subject for inspiring whatever merit there is to his verse. **Line 1,** *want subject to invent*: lack things to write about. **Line 3,** *argument*: ie, the subject of the verse. **Line 4,** *vulgar paper*: common writing; *rehearse*: repeat. **Line 6,** *invention*: creativity. **Line 9,** *Be thou the tenth Muse*: Classical tradition spoke of Nine Muses who presided over the Arts, with Erato being the Muse of lyric poetry. The verse postulates its subject as the tenth, and being more glorious than the others. **Line 12,** *Eternal numbers*: immortal poetry.

39

O, how thy worth with manners may I sing
When thou art all the better part of me?
What can mine own praise to mine own self bring?
And what is't but mine own when I praise thee?
Even for this, let us divided live,
And our dear love lose name of single one,
That by this separation I may give
That due to thee, which thou deservest alone.
O absence, what a torment wouldst thou prove
Were it not thy sour leisure gave sweet leave
To entertain the time with thoughts of love,
Which time and thoughts so sweetly doth deceive,
  And that thou teachest how to make one twain,
  By praising him here who doth hence remain!

NOTES: The poet notes that their separation gives him the leisure to contemplate the subject's worth, and the love they share. **Line 1,** *with manners*: ie, with all due modesty. **Line 5,** *Even for this*: for this reason. **Line 12,** *deceive*: beguile. **Lines 13-14,** *how to make...doth hence remain*: ie, though parted, we remain united in thought and spirit.

40

Take all my loves, my love; yea, take them all.
What hast thou then, more than thou hadst before?
No love, my love, that thou mayst true love call;
All mine was thine before thou hadst this more.
Then if, for my love, thou my love receivest,
I cannot blame thee for my love thou usest,
But yet be blamed, if thou thyself deceivest
By willful taste of what thyself refusest.
I do forgive thy robbery, gentle thief,
Although thou steal thee all my poverty.
And yet love knows it is a greater grief
To bear love's wrong than hate's known injury.
   Lascivious grace, in whom all ill well shows,
   Kill me with spites; yet, we must not be foes.

NOTES: In this sonnet, and the next two as well, the poet is chastising the subject for seducing the poet's own mistress. **Line 4,** *mine was thine...this more*: you had my own love before taking these additional favors. **Line 5,** *Then if...my love receivest*: if you took my mistress because you love me. **Line 6,** *for my love thou usest*: for dallying with my own mistress. **Line 8,** *willful taste*: savoring or enjoying. **Line 10,** *thou steal thee all my poverty*: you take what little I have. **Line 11,** *grief*: sorrow. **Line 13,** *Lascivious grace*: seductive beauty. **Line 14,** *spites*: annoyances; vexations.

41

Those petty wrongs that liberty commits,
When I am sometime absent from thy heart,
Thy beauty and thy years full well befits,
For still temptation follows where thou art.
Gentle thou art, and therefore to be won;
Beauteous thou art, therefore to be assailed.
And when a woman woos, what woman's son
Will sourly leave her till she have prevailed?
Aye me! but yet thou might'st my seat forbear,
And chide thy beauty, and thy straying youth,
Who lead thee in their riot even there
Where thou art forced to break a twofold truth—
  Hers by thy beauty tempting her to thee;
  Thine, by thy beauty being false to me.

NOTES: Continuing the complaints in the previous sonnet, the poet notes that the subject has betrayed two people—the poet, as well as the mistress. **Line 1,** *petty wrongs*: small offenses; *liberty*: licentiousness or wantonness. **Line 5,** *gentle*: well-born, ie, of proper birth. **Line 8,** *sourly*: peevishly, gruffly. **Line 9,** *seat*: place. **Line 11,** *riot*: licentiousness or debauchery. **Line 12,** *truth*: pledge or loyalty.

42

That thou hast her, it is not all my grief,
And yet it may be said I loved her dearly.
That she hath thee is of my wailing chief,
A loss in love that touches me more nearly.
Loving offenders, thus I will excuse ye:
Thou dost love her, because thou knowst I love her;
And for my sake even so doth she abuse me,
Suffering my friend for my sake to approve her.
If I lose thee, my loss is my love's gain,
And losing her, my friend hath found that loss.
Both find each other, and I lose both twain,
And both for my sake lay on me this cross.
 But here's the joy—my friend and I are one.
 Sweet flattery! then she loves but me alone.

NOTES: Concluding the saga of the licentious rivalry, the poet tries to rationalize the betrayal by pretending that the mistress and the subject are dallying with each other only to express their love for the poet. **Line 3,** *of my wailing chief*: my biggest sorrow. **Line 4,** *nearly*: closely or acutely. **Line 7,** *abuse*: injure or wound. **Line 8,** *Suffering*: allowing; *approve*: tempt, or make a trial of (ie, try her out). **Line 9,** *my love's*: my mistress's. **Line 10,** *found that loss*: recovered what I have lost. **Line 12,** *lay on me this cross*: make me suffer this burden.

43

When most I wink, then do mine eyes best see,
For all the day they view things unrespected.
But when I sleep, in dreams they look on thee
And, darkly bright, are bright in dark directed.
Then thou, whose shadow shadows doth make bright,
How would thy shadow's form form happy show
To the clear day with thy much clearer light,
When to unseeing eyes thy shade shines so!
How would, I say, mine eyes be blessèd made
By looking on thee in the living day,
When in dead night thy fair imperfect shade
Through heavy sleep on sightless eyes doth stay?
  All days are nights to see till I see thee,
  And nights bright days when dreams do show thee me.

NOTES: Separated from the subject, the poet remarks that he can see better asleep that he does awake—though he would rather see the subject in person than merely in his dreams. **Line 1,** *wink*: sleep. **Line 2,** *unrespected*: unseen or unnoticed. **Line 4,** *darkly bright*: glowing behind my eyelids; *bright in dark directed*: guided through the darkness by your brightness. **Line 5,** *shadow*: image or appearance. **Line 6,** *shadow's form*: the physical reality behind the shadow; *form happy show*: make a joyful appearance. **Line 8:** *thy shade*: your image or appearance. **Line 11,** *they fair imperfect shade*: your pleasing though imaginary image.

44

If the dull substance of my flesh were thought,
Injurious distance should not stop my way.
For then, despite of space, I would be brought
From limits far remote, where thou dost stay.
No matter, then, although my foot did stand
Upon the farthest earth removed from thee,
For nimble thought can jump both sea and land
As soon as think the place where he would be.
But ah! thought kills me, that I am not thought
To leap large lengths of miles when thou art gone,
But that so much of earth and water wrought
I must attend time's leisure with my moan,
   Receiving naught by elements so slow
   But heavy tears, badges of either's woe.

NOTES: In this poem and the next one, the poet reflects upon the benefits of being mere thought, rather than composed of the "four elements." **Line 1,** *dull substance*: ie, earth and water, the "dull elements" of the four elements of Aristotle, which are also important in astrology. This sonnet and the one following put forth the imagery of the four elements: earth, water, air, and fire. **Line 2,** *stop my way*: impede or block my path. **Line 4,** *limits*: regions. **Line 9:** *thought kills me*: the idea makes me despair. **Line 11,** *wrought*: shaped or made. **Line 12,** *attend time's leisure*: await the passage of time; *moan*: lamentation. **Line 13,** *elements so slow*: earth and water were considered the "heavy" elements, as opposed to air and fire.

45

The other two, slight air and purging fire,
Are both with thee, wherever I abide.
The first my thought, the other my desire,
These present-absent with swift motion slide.
For when these quicker elements are gone
In tender embassy of love to thee,
My life, being made of four, with two alone
Sinks down to death, oppressed with melancholy,
Until life's composition be recured
By those swift messengers returned from thee
Who, even but now, come back again, assured
Of they fair health, recounting it to me.
   This told, I joy; but then, no longer glad,
   I send them back again, and straight grow sad.

NOTES: Continuing the theme from the previous sonnet. **Line 1,** *other two*: ie, the other two elements of Greek science and astrology. **Line 5,** *quicker elements*: ie, air and fire, which were less heavy than earth and water. **Line 6,** *embassy*: mission or message. **Line 7,** *made of four*: comprised of the four elements. **Line 9,** *Until life's composition be recured*: until all four elements are restored or reunited.

46

Mine eye and heart are at a mortal war:
How to divide the conquest of thy sight.
Mine eye, my heart thy picture's sight would bar;
My heart, mine eye the freedom of that right.
My heart doth plead that thou in him dost lie,
A closet never pierced with crystal eyes.
But, the defendant doth that plea deny,
And says, in him thy fair appearance lies.
To 'cide this title is impanelèd
A quest of thoughts, all tenants to the heart,
And by their verdict is determined
The clear eye's moiety and the dear heart's part
  As thus: mine eye's due is thy outward part,
  And my heart's right, thy inward love of heart.

NOTES: Discourses on the divide between the eyes and the heart being a common theme in Renaissance poetry, the next two sonnets form a witty dispute between the two—perhaps by way of a thank-you note the poet is writing for the gift of a portrait. **Line 1,** *mortal*: deadly. **Line 2,** *How to divide...of thy sight*: How to share the right to gaze upon your picture. **Line 6,** *closet*: a cabinet for storing valuables, or a small private room. **Lines 9-10,** *To 'cide this title...a quest of thoughts*: A jury is chosen to decide the question. **Line 12,** *moiety*: fair share.

47

Betwixt mine eye and heart a league is took,
And each doth good turns now unto the other.
When that mine eye is famished for a look,
Or heart in love with sighs himself doth smother,
With my love's picture then my eye doth feast,
And to the painted banquet bids my heart.
Another time mine eye is my heart's guest,
And in his thoughts of love doth share a part.
So, either by thy picture or my love,
Thyself away art present still with me,
For thou no farther than my thoughts canst move,
And I am still with them, and they with thee.
  Or, if they sleep, thy picture in my sight
  Awakes my heart to heart's and eye's delight.

NOTES: Continuing the theme from the preceding sonnet, after the dispute is resolved the heart and eyes become reconciled, each thereby doubling its allotment by sharing the other's portion. **Line 1,** *a league is took*: an agreement is reached. **Line 11,** *no*: the original text reads "nor."

48

How careful was I when I took my way,
Each trifle under truest bars to thrust,
That to my use it might unusèd stay
From hands of falsehood, in sure wards of trust!
But thou, to whom my jewels trifles are,
Most worthy of comfort, now my greatest grief,
Thou, best of dearest and mine only care,
Art left the prey of every vulgar thief.
Thee, have I not locked up in any chest,
Save where thou art not, though I feel thou art
Within the gentle closure of my breast,
From whence at pleasure thou mayst come and part.
    And even thence thou wilt be stol'n, I fear,
    For truth proves thievish for a prize so dear.

NOTES: In this sonnet, the poet contrasts the difficulty of safeguarding valuable possessions with the impossibility of securing someone's love. (It also shows Shakespeare's ability to mask his bawdy sense of humor through seemingly innocuous wordplay). **Line 1,** *took my way*: set out upon my journey. **Line 2,** *truest*: safest; most secure. **Line 4,** *hands of falsehood*: ie, thieves; *wards*: guards, or a place that can be locked for safekeeping. **Line 5,** *to whom*: in comparison to whom. **Line 6,** *Most worthy comfort*: ie, you, who are my greatest joy. **Line 7,** *mine only care*: my main concern. **Line 8,** *vulgar*: common. **Line 11,** *closure*: enclosure. **Line 12:** *at pleasure*: at will.

49

Against that time, if ever that time come,
When I shall see thee frown on my defects;
When as thy love hath cast his utmost sum,
Called to that audit by advised respects—
Against that time, when thou shalt strangely pass
And scarcely greet me with that sun, thine eye;
When love, converted from the thing it was,
Shall reasons find of settled gravity—
Against that time do I ensconce me here,
Within the knowledge of mine own desert,
And this my hand against myself uprear
To guard the lawful reasons on thy part.
   To leave poor me, thou hast the strength of laws,
   Since why to love I can allege no cause.

NOTES: Here, the poet is trying to steel himself against the day when his subject, mindful at last of the poet's many defects, rejects him. **Line 3,** *cast his utmost sum*: balanced all accounts. **Line 4,** *advised respects*: deliberate consideration. **Line 5,** *strangely pass*: pass like a stranger. **Line 8,** *of settled gravity*: of outward respectability. **Line 9,** *ensconce*: fortify. **Line 10,** *mine own desert*: what I deserve. **Line 11,** *my hand against myself uprear*: ie, testify against myself (as a witness raising his hand to swear an oath to tell the truth). **Line 14,** *allege*: plead as an excuse (continuing the courtroom image).

50

How heavy do I journey on the way,
When what I seek, my weary travel's end,
Doth teach that ease and that repose to say
"Thus far the miles are measured from thy friend!"
The beast that bears me, tired with my woe,
Plods duly on, to bear that weight in me,
As if by some instínct the wretch did know
His rider loved not speed, being made from thee.
The bloody spur cannot provoke him on
That sometimes anger thrusts into his hide,
Which, heavily, he answers with a groan
More sharp to me than spurring to his side,
   For that same groan doth put this in my mind:
   My grief lies onward, and my joy behind.

NOTES: This and the next sonnet compare the heavy slowness of departing from the subject (in Sonnet 50) with the speed of his return (in Sonnet 51). **Line 1,** *heavy*: sorrowfully. **Line 6,** *duly*: some authorities read the text as "dully," which finds an echo in Line 2 of the next sonnet. (The lack of standardized spelling in Elizabethan England gave Shakespeare an artistic license which can give modern academics an almost infinite universe of possibilities to quibble over); *to bear that weight*: ie, the weight of my woe. **Line 8,** *being made from thee*: taking me away from you.

51

Thus, can my love excuse the slow offense
Of my dull bearer, when from thee I speed.
From where thou art, why should I haste me thence?
Till I return, of posting is no need.
O, what excuse will my poor beast then find
When swift extremity can seem but slow?
Then should I spur, though mounted on the wind,
In wingèd speed no motion shall I know.
Then can no horse with my desire keep pace,
Therefore desire, of perfect'st love being made,
Shall neigh no dull flesh in his fiery race,
But love, for love, thus shall excuse my jade:
   Since from thee going he went willful slow,
   Towards thee I'll run, and give him leave to go.

NOTES: While the poor horse of the preceeding sonnet is probably finding the impatience of the returning rider to be a source of aggravation, the poet appears to recognize that the horse will never keep pace with his desire to return. **Line 1,** *slow offense*: the offense of slowness. **Line 2,** *my dull bearer*: ie, my hapless horse. **Line 4,** *posting*: riding swiftly. **Line 6,** *swift extremity*: extreme speed. **Line 11,** *neigh...in his fiery race*. Lines 9-14 seem destined to give editors fits, and is not helped by the fact that a key phrase in the original—"naigh noe dull flesh"—is in many ways incomprehensible to the modern reader. Though perhaps risky to rule out a bawdy Shakespearean pun, most appear to regard the phrase as contrasting the dull flesh of the horse with the fiery flesh of desire. (It is also quite possible that it was simply a misprint in the original...nobody thought to ask Shakespeare at the time...and modern scholars are often more comfortable trying to discern sense out of the lines than admitting that they really have no clue what they might mean). **Line 12,** *jade*: poor-spirited horse. **Line 14,** *go*: walk.

52

So am I as the rich, whose blessèd key
Can bring him to his sweet uplockèd treasure,
The which he will not every hour survey,
For blunting the fine point of seldom pleasure.
Therefore are feasts so solemn and so rare,
Since, seldom coming in the long year, set
Like stones of worth they thinly placèd are,
Or captain jewels in the carcanet.
So is the time that keeps you as my chest,
Or as the wardrobe, which the robe doth hide
To make some special instant special blest,
By new unfolding his imprisoned pride.
    Blessèd are you, whose worthiness gives scope:
    Being had, to triumph—being lacked, to hope.

NOTES: The playfully bawdy poet notes that the infrequency of his meeting with the subject makes their time together all the more pleasurable in that, like fine jewels, they are more precious for their rarity. **Line 4,** *For blunting*: for fear of blunting. **Line 7,** *stones of worth*: valuable gems; *thinly placèd*: spaced at wide intervals. **Line 8,** *captain*: chief; *carcanet*: necklace. **Line 9:** *keeps you as my chest*: maintains you as my treasure chest. **Line 10,** *wardrobe*: a rich man's room where valuable clothing is kept under guard. **Line 12:** *new unfolding*: newly revealing; *imprisoned pride*: the pride of the hidden collection of treasure.

53

What is your substance, whereof are you made,
That millions of strange shadows on you tend,
Since every one, hath every one, one shade,
And you, but one, can every shadow lend.
Describe Adonis, and the counterfeit
Is poorly imitated after you.
On Helen's cheek all art of beauty set,
And you in Grecian tires are painted new.
Speak of the spring and foison of the year,
The one doth shadow of your beauty show,
The other as your bounty doth appear,
And you in every blessèd shape we know.
　In all external grace you have some part,
　But you like none, none you, for constant heart.

NOTES: The poet remarks that the subject makes other symbols of beauty—such as Adonis, or Helen of Troy—pale in comparison. **Line 2,** *shadows*: reflections; *on you tend*: serve or follow you. **Line 4,** *but*: only; *every shadow lend*: be the source of all other images. **Line 5,** *Adonis*: the beloved of Venus; *counterfeit*: copy, or portrait. **Line 7,** *On Helen's cheek...beauty set*: render the image of Helen of Troy as skillfully as possible...even if artists need to touch her up a bit. **Line 8,** *Grecian tires*: Grecian attire, ie, clad like a Greek noblewoman (rather than a Greek bearing radial white walls. Shakespeare did, after all, write in the days before used car salesmen). **Line 9,** *foison*: the season of plenty, ie, the fall, or harvest season. **Line 10,** *shadow*: image. **Line 12,** *And you*: and you appear. **Line 14,** *you like none, none you*: you are like no others, and no others can compare to you.

54

O, how much more doth beauty beauteous seem
By that sweet ornament which truth doth give!
The rose looks fair, but fairer we it deem
For that sweet odor which doth in it live.
The canker blooms have full as deep a dye
As the perfumèd tincture of the roses,
Hang on such thorns, and play as wantonly
When summer's breath their maskèd buds discloses.
But, for their virtue only is their show,
They live unwooed, and unrespected fade,
Die to themselves. Sweet roses do not so;
Of their sweet deaths are sweetest odors made.
   And so of you, beauteous and lovely youth;
   When that shall fade, my verse distills your truth.

NOTES: Noting that the essence of flowers is distilled into perfume, the poet suggests that the essence of the subject is distilled in his poetry. **Line 2,** *By*: through; *truth*: constancy. **Line 5,** *canker blooms*: wild (and odorless) roses, as contrasted with the "perfumèd" roses of the next line. **Line 6,** *tincture*: color or hue. **Line 8,** *their maskèd buds discloses*: opens their blossoms. **Line 9,** *for*: because, since. **Line 10,** *unrespected*: unnoticed, ignored. **Line 12,** Of their sweet deaths... odors made: when sweet roses die, their essence is made into perfume. **Line 14,** *fade, my*: many editors, following the original Quarto, read the line as "vade," or depart, and some retain the original "by" for "my." (The quaint Elizabethan typesetting—where s's look like f's, and u's and v's often appear where one least expects them—perplexes many of us).

55

Not marble, nor the gilded monuments
Of princes, shall outlive this powerful rhyme.
But you shall shine more bright in these contents
Than unswept stone, besmeared with sluttish time.
When wasteful war shall statues overturn,
And broils root out the work of masonry,
Nor Mars his sword nor war's quick fire shall burn
The living record of your memory.
'Gainst death and all oblivious enmity
Shall you pace forth; your praise shall still find room,
Even in the eyes of all posterity
That wear this world out to the ending doom.
  So, till the judgment that yourself arise,
  You live in this, and dwell in lovers' eyes.

NOTES: The continuation of the theme of the subject's preservation in verse from the couplet of the last sonnet suggests that the two were probably linked. **Line 4,** *unswept stone*: ie, a dusty stone slab covering a grave on a church floor; *sluttish*: dirty or slovenly. **Line 6,** *broils*: conflicts, melees. **Line 9,** *all oblivious enmity*: unmindful hostility or indifference. **Line 10,** *still*: always. **Line 12-13,** *ending doom, judgment*: ie, Judgment Day.

56

Sweet love, renew thy force; be it not said
Thy edge should blunter be than appetite,
Which but today by feeding is allayed,
Tomorrow sharpened in his former might.
So, love, be thou; although today thou fill
Thy hungry eyes even till they wink with fullness,
Tomorrow see again, and do not kill
The spirit of love with a perpetual dullness.
Let this sad interim like the ocean be
Which parts the shore, where two contracted new
Come daily to the banks, that, when they see
Return of love, more blest may be the view.
    Else call it winter, which being full of care
    Makes summer's welcome thrice more wished, more rare.

NOTES: The poet remarks that the separation of lovers may increase the intensity of their devotion to each other. **Line 4,** *his*: its (ie, appetitie's). **Line 6,** *wink*: close. **Line 8,** *dullness*: apathy. **Line 10,** *contracted new*: newly engaged or betrothed. **Line 14,** *rare*: splendid, as well as uncommon.

57

Being your slave, what should I do but tend
Upon the hours and times of your desire?
I have no precious time at all to spend,
Nor services to do, till you require.
Nor dare I chide the world without end hour
Whilst I, my sovereign, watch the clock for you,
Nor think the bitterness of absence sour
When you have bid your servant once adieu.
Nor dare I question, with my jealous thought,
Where you may be, or your affairs suppose,
But, like a sad slave, stay and think of nought
Save where you are, how happy you make those.
  So true a fool is love that in your will,
  Though you do any thing, he thinks no ill.

NOTES: The next two sonnets cast the subject and poet in the roles of master and slave. **Lines 1-2,** *tend...your desire*: await your pleasure. **Line 5,** *world without end*: endless. **Line 7,** *bitterness*: anguish, sorrow. **Line 10,** *suppose*: guess. **Line 10-11,** *think of nought...happy you make those*: think of nothing except how happy you make those around you. **Line 13,** *true*: faithful; *will*: whim (or desire), or Will, the poet.

58

That god forbid, that made me first your slave,
I should in thought control your times of pleasure,
Or at your hand th' account of hours to crave,
Being your vassal, bound to stay your leisure!
O, let me suffer, being at your beck,
The imprisoned absence of your liberty.
And patience tame to sufferance bide each check,
Without accusing you of injury.
Be where you list, your charter is so strong
That you yourself may privilege your time
To what you will; to you it doth belong,
Yourself to pardon of self-doing crime.
   I am to wait, though waiting so be hell,
   Not blame your pleasure, be it ill or well.

NOTES: Continuing the imagery of servitude from the previous sonnet. **Line 2,** *in thought*: in my imagination; times of pleasure: recreational activities (the allusion here, and in the previous sonnet, intimate that those activities likely include the bedroom). **Lines 5-6,** *let me suffer...absence of your liberty*: being yours to command, your absence makes me a prisoner. **Line 7,** *tame to sufferance*: enured to the point of acquiesence; *bide each check*: endure every reprimand or rebuke. **Line 9,** *where you list*: wherever you want to be, *charter*: acknowledged right. **Line 10,** *privilege*: authorize. **Line 12,** *self-doing*: done by, or to, yourself. **Line 13,** *wait*: await, or serve. **Lines 13-14**: the image and wordplay apply equally to a servant awaiting his master's return, and a lover impatiently waiting for his absent mistress.

59

If there be nothing new, but that which is
Hath been before, how are our brains beguiled,
Which, laboring for invention, bear amiss
The second burden of a former child?
O, that recórd could with a backward look,
Even of five hundred courses of the sun,
Show me your image in some antique book,
Since mind at first in character was done,
That I might see what the old world could say
To this composèd wonder of your frame,
Whether we are mended, or whether better they,
Or whether revolution be the same.
  O, sure I am, the wits of former days
  To subjects worse have given admiring praise.

NOTES: This sonnet plays with the proverb that "there is nothing new under the sun." **Line 2,** *beguiled*: deceived. **Line 3,** *invention*: something new. **Lines 3-4,** *laboring for invention...a former child*: the line carries images of childbirth gone awry (laboring for invention, bear amiss...second burden), but the essence is taking as new ideas which have already been expressed by someone else. **Line 5,** *recórd*: written account; memory. **Line 6,** *courses of the sun*: years. **Line 8,** *mind at first in character was done*: since thoughts were first recorded in writing. **Line 10,** *composèd wonder*: constructed marvel. **Line 11,** *mended*: improved. **Line 12,** *whether revolution be the same*: whether each cycle (of history, or the earth) keeps things mostly as they are. **Line 13,** *wits*: clever writers.

60

Like as the waves make towards the pebbled shore,
So do our minutes hasten to their end,
Each changing place with that which goes before,
In sequent toil all forwards do contend.
Nativity, once in the main of light,
Crawls to maturity, wherewith being crowned,
Crookèd eclipses 'gainst his glory fight,
And time that gave doth now his gift confound.
Time doth transfix the flourish set on youth,
And delves the parallels in beauty's brow,
Feeds on the rarities of nature's truth,
And nothing stands but for his scythe to mow.
   And yet to times, in hope, my verse shall stand,
   Praising thy worth, despite his cruel hand.

NOTES: This sonnet recalls the cycle of life, from birth to death, expressing the hope that the poem will keep the subject's beauty alive. **Line 4,** *sequent:* successive. **Line 5,** *Nativity:* birth; *main of light:* light of day. **Line 7,** *Crookèd:* bending with age. **Line 9,** *transfix:* pierce; *flourish:* blossom. **Line 10,** *delves the parallels:* plows the wrinkles (parallels are, literally, military trenches dug on a battlefield). **Line 11,** *rarities:* wonders. **Line 12,** *scythe:* the image is of Father Time (or the grim reaper) harvesting the season's bounty.

61

Is it thy will thy image should keep open
My heavy eyelids to the weary night?
Dost thou desire my slumbers should be broken,
While shadows like to thee do mock my sight?
Is it thy spirit that thou send'st from thee
So far from home into my deeds to pry,
To find out shames and idle hours in me,
The scope and tenor of thy jealousy?
O, no! thy love, though much, is not so great.
It is my love that keeps mine eye awake,
Mine own true love that doth my rest defeat,
To play the watchman ever for thy sake.
  For thee watch I, whilst thou dost wake elsewhére,
  From me far off, with others all too near.

NOTES: In this sonnet, the subject's image, and the poet's own jealousy, is
keeping the poet awake. **Line 4,** *shadows like to thee*: images that look like you **Line
7,** *shames*: shameful deeds; *idle hours*: wasted time. **Line 8,** *the scope and tenor*: the aim
and intent; *jealousy*: suspicion. **Line 13,** *For thee...wake elsewhere*: I stay awake worrying
while you are off reveling.

62

Sin of self-love possesseth all mine eye,
And all my soul, and all my every part,
And for this sin there is no remedy;
It is so grounded inward in my heart.
Methinks no face so gracious is as mine,
No shape so true, no truth of such account.
And, for myself, mine own worth do define,
As I all other in all worths surmount.
But when my glass shows me myself, indeed,
Beated and chopped with tanned antiquity,
Mine own self-love quite contrary I read.
Self so self-loving were iniquity.
  'Tis thee, myself, that for myself I praise,
  Painting my age with beauty of thy days.

NOTES: Chiding himself for his own vanity, the poet admits that the "self" he holds in esteem is really the subject—his alter ego. **Line 5,** *Methinks*: it seems to me. **Line 6,** *true*: perfect. **Line 9,** *glass*: mirror. **Line 10,** *Beated and chopped*: Overpowered and roughened; *antiquity*: old age. **Line 11,** *quite contrary I read*: I see in the opposite way (as a mirror reflects an inverted image). **Line 12,** *Self so...were iniquity*: to love such a self would be sinful. **Line 13,** *'Tis thee, myself*: It is you, my second self. **Line 14,** *Painting...of thy days*: curing the defects of my age with my descriptions of your youthful beauty.

63

Against my love shall be, as I am now,
With Time's injurious hand crushed and o'er-worn,
When hours have drained his blood and filled his brow
With lines and wrinkles; when his youthful morn
Hath traveled on to age's steepy night,
And all those beauties, whereof now he's king,
Are vanishing or vanished out of sight,
Stealing away the treasure of his spring.
For such a time do I now fortify
Against confounding age's cruel knife,
That he shall never cut from memory
My sweet love's beauty, though my lover's life.
  His beauty shall in these black lines be seen,
    And they shall live, and he in them still green.

NOTES: This sonnet, and the two following, appear to continue the imagery of time eroding beauty. **Line 1,** *Against*: Anticipating the day when.... **Line 5,** *steepy*: steep, precipitous. **Line 10,** *Against*: in opposition to, opposing; *confounding*: destructive. **Line 11,** *he*: ie, Time; *memory*: history, or common memory. **Line 14,** *in them still green*: be ever young in these verses.

64

When I have seen by time's fell hand defaced
The rich proud cost of outworn buried age;
When sometime lofty towers I see down-razed,
And brass eternal slave to mortal rage;
When I have seen the hungry ocean gain
Advantage on the kingdom of the shore,
And the firm soil win of the watery main,
Increasing store with loss and loss with store;
When I have seen such interchange of state,
Or state itself confounded to decay,
Ruin hath taught me thus to ruminate
That time will come and take my love away.
   This thought is as a death, which cannot choose
   But weep to have that which it fears to lose.

NOTES: Continuing the theme of time destroying beauty, the poet notes the
effects of age on buildings and shorelines. **Line 1,** *fell*: cruel or ruthless. **Line 2,** *The
rich proud cost of outworn buried age*: The fancy and expensive memorials of bygone
eras. **Line 3,** *sometime*: at one time; formerly. **Line 4,** *brass eternal*: indestructible
brass; *mortal rage*: human fury or destructiveness. **Lines 5-8:** territory lost to and
reclaimed from the sea was a matter of interest in Elizabethan times. **Line 6,**
Advantage on: superiority over. **Line 7,** *wat'ry main*: ocean. **Line 9,** *state*: condition.
Line 10, *state*: pomp and splendor; the ruling power.

65

Since brass, nor stone, nor earth, nor boundless sea,
But sad mortality o'er-sways their power,
How with this rage shall beauty hold a plea,
Whose action is no stronger than a flower?
O, how shall summer's honey breath hold out
Against the wrackful siege of battering days
When rocks impregnable are not so stout,
Nor gates of steel so strong, but time decays?
O fearful meditation! where, alack,
Shall time's best jewel from time's chest lie hid?
Or what strong hand can hold his swift foot back?
Or who his spoil or beauty can forbid?
    O, none, unless this miracle have might—
    That in black ink my love may still shine bright.

NOTES: Seeing that beauty is helpless to stop the decaying power of Time, the poet concludes that the only real defense is poetry. **Lines 1-2,** *Since brass nor stone...But sad mortality...their power...*: Because time overcomes all things. **Line 3, *with*:** against.; *rage*: lustful violence; *hold a plea*: plead its case; prevail in court. **Line 6,** *wrackful*: destructive. **Line 7, *stout*:** strong; sturdy. **Line 10:** *Time's best jewel*: the loveliest thing in all creation; *Time's chest*: as "chest" would be a "treasure chest," Time's chest would be a coffin. **Line 12,** *spoil*: ruin or destruction. In the original Quarto text, the line reads "spoil or beauty," which most editors alter "spoil of beauty" because the "his" in Line 11 is usually take to be Time's. If we take it to mean the subject, however, we could read the original line as asking "who can stop either his beauty or its destruction?" **Lines 13-14,** *unless this miracle...that in black ink my love may still shine bright*: my love's only hope for immortality lies in my verse.

66

Tired with all these, for restful death I cry:
As, to behold desert a beggar born,
And needy nothing trimmed in jollity;
And purest faith unhappily forsworn,
And gilded honor shamefully misplaced;
And maiden virtue rudely strumpeted,
And right perfection wrongfully disgraced;
And strength by limping sway disablèd,
And art made tongue-tied by authority;
And folly, doctor-like, controlling skill,
And simple truth miscalled simplicity;
And captive good attending captain ill.
   Tired with all these, from these would I be gone,
   Save that, to die, I leave my love alone.

NOTES: Recounting the worldly woes that would make death a welcome relief, the poet observes that this would leave the subject alone, giving the poet a reason to keep living. **Line 1,** *with all these*: with all that follow; *desert*: a worthy person. **Line 3,** *needy nothing trimmed in jollity*: a worthless fop clad in fine clothes. **Line 4,** *unhappily forsworn*: regrettably abandoned. **Line 5,** *gilded honor*: golden titles; *misplaced*: given to undeserving recipients. **Line 7,** *true*: real or genuine. **Line 8,** *strength by limping sway*: weak or ineffectual authority. **Line 9,** *art made tongue-tied by authority*: skillfulness bowing to patronage or censorship. **Line 10,** *doctorlike*: with scholarly pretensions. **Line 11,** *simple truth*: plain honesty; *simplicity*: silliness or foolishness. **Line 12,** *attending*: serving.

67

Ah! wherefore with infection should he live,
And with his presence grace impiety,
That sin by him advantage should achieve
And lace itself with his society?
Why should false painting imitate his cheek,
And steal dead seeing of his living hue?
Why should poor beauty indirectly seek
Roses of shadow, since his rose is true?
Why should he live, now Nature bankrupt is,
Beggared of blood to blush through lively veins?
For she hath no exchequer now but his,
And, proud of many, lives upon his gains.
   O, him she stores, to show what wealth she had
   In days long since, before these last so bad.

NOTES: Lamenting that the subject's beauty seems to give legitimacy to the corruption of the age, the poet concludes that Nature is choosing to use the subject as a reminder of better times. **Line 1,** *wherefore with infection*: why in these corrupt (or plague-ridden) times. **Line 2,** *grace*: adorn. **Line 4,** *lace*: adorn or ornament. **Line 5,** *false painting*: portraiture, or cosmetics. **Line 6,** *steal dead seeing*: make an inanimate image. **Line 7,** *poor*: inferior; *indirectly*: dishonestly, or through use of an intermediary. **Line 8,** *Roses of shadow*: ie, false or imitated color. **Line 10:** *beggared*: deprived or destitute. **Line 11,** *she hath no exchequer now but his*: he is now the only specimen of beauty that she (ie, Nature) has left. **Line 13,** *stores*: keeps or preserves.

68

Thus is his cheek the map of days outworn,
When beauty lived and died as flowers do now,
Before the bastard signs of fair were born,
Or durst inhabit on a living brow;
Before the golden tresses of the dead,
The right of sepulchers, were shorn away
To live a second life on second head,
Ere beauty's dead fleece made another gay.
In him those holy antique hours are seen
Without all ornament, itself and true,
Making no summer of another's green,
Robbing no old to dress his beauty new.
   And him, as for a map, doth Nature store
   To show false art what beauty was of yore.

NOTES: Continuing the theme of the previous sonnet, the poet compares the subject's natural beauty against the artificiality of those who rely upon cosmetics. **Line 1,** *map*: embodiment; *days outworm*: bygone days. **Line 3,** *bastard signs of fair*: counterfeit beauty—ie, cosmetics. **Line 5,** *the golden tresses of the dead*: In Shakespeare's day, the hair on blond wigs was often taken from corpses. See, Harrison, *Shakespeare: The Complete Works,* p 599n. (Those with blond hair apparently had more fun in Shakespeare's day as well as our own, and the well-to-do mostly likely reasoned that corpses no longer needed theirs). **Line 10,** *itself and true*: ie, pure, unaltered. **Line 13,** *him as for a map doth Nature store*: ie, Nature uses him as a pattern.

69

Those parts of thee that the world's eye doth view
Want nothing that the thought of hearts can mend.
All tongues, the voice of souls, give thee that due,
Uttering bare truth, even so as foes commend.
Thy outward thus with outward praise is crowned,
But those same tongues that give thee so thine own
In other accents do this praise confound
By seeing farther than the eye hath shown.
They look into the beauty of thy mind,
And that, in guess, they measure by thy deeds.
Then, churls, their thoughts, although their eyes were kind,
To thy fair flower add the rank smell of weeds.
  But why thy odor matcheth not thy show,
  The soil is this, that thou dost common grow.

NOTES: The poet warns that some who praise the subject's outward beauty in public speak quite differently in private, owing to the subject's having become "common." **Line 2,** *thought of hearts*: heart's desires. **Line 4,** *even so as foes commend*: as even an enemy would acknowledge. **Line 5,** *outward praise*: public praise. **Line 7,** *other accents*: language differing in tone. **Line 8,** *farther than the eye hath shown*: looking deeper than the surface. **Line 10,** *in guess*: by estimation. **Lines 11-12,** *churls*: rude or surly people; *although their eyes were kind...add the rank smell of weeds*: ie, those who are jealous of your beauty inwardly impute ill motives to your actions and think ill of you . **Line 14,** *soil:* stain or imperfection, also, to resolve; *thou dost common grow*: you are open (ie, common) to all.

70

That thou art blamed shall not be thy defect,
For slander's mark was ever yet the fair.
The ornament of beauty is suspéct,
A crow that flies in heaven's sweetest air.
So thou be good, slander doth but approve
Thy worth the greater, being wooed of time;
For canker vice the sweetest buds doth love,
And thou present'st a pure unstainèd prime.
Thou hast passed by the ambush of young days,
Either not assailed, or victor being charged.
Yet this thy praise cannot be so thy praise,
To tie up envy evermore enlarged.
    If some suspect of ill masked not thy show,
    Then thou alone kingdoms of hearts shouldst owe.

NOTES: Here, the poet reassures the subject that beauty often provokes attacks, due to jealousy. **Line 1,** *shall not be thy defect*: is no fault of yours. **Line 2,** *mark*: target. **Line 3,** *suspéct*: suspicion. **Line 5,** *So*: as long as; *approve*: prove. **Line 7,** *canker vice*: like a canker, vice.... **Line 8,** *unstainèd prime*: unblemished prime of life. **Line 9,** *ambush of young days*: pitfalls of youth. **Line 10,** *victor being charged*: prevailing against attack. **Line 12,** *enlarged*: at large; free to come and go. **Line 13,** *suspect*: suspicions; *masked*: hid or concealed. **Line 14:** *alone*: uniquely; *owe*: own.

71

No longer mourn for me when I am dead
Than you shall hear the surly sullen bell
Give warning to the world that I am fled
From this vile world, with vilest worms to dwell.
Nay, if you read this line, remember not
The hand that writ it; for I love you so
That I in your sweet thoughts would be forgot,
If thinking on me then should make you woe.
O, if, I say, you look upon this verse
When I, perhaps, compounded am with clay,
Do not so much as my poor name rehearse,
But let your love even with my life decay,
   Lest the wise world should look into your moan
   And mock you with me, after I am gone.

NOTES: Considering the question of his own mortality, the poet advises the subject to forget him once he has passed away. **Line 2,** *Than:* some editors retain the original "then," since Elizabethans used the two spellings interchangeably for both words; *sullen bell:* the bell tolling for a funeral. **Line 3,** *warning:* the funeral bell not only served as notice of the departed, but also as a reminder of our mortality. **Line 8,** *make you woe:* cause you grief. **Line 10,** *compounded am with clay:* have returned to the earth. **Line 11,** *rehearse:* repeat. **Line 13,** *look into your moan:* seek to learn the cause of your grief.

72

O, lest the world should task you to recite
What merit lived in me that you should love
After my death, dear love, forget me quite.
For you in me can nothing worthy prove,
Unless you would devise some virtuous lie
To do more for me than mine own desert,
And hang more praise upon deceasèd I
Than niggard truth would willingly impart.
O, lest your true love may seem false in this,
That you for love speak well of me untrue,
My name be buried where my body is,
And live no more to shame nor me nor you.
  For I am shamed by that which I bring forth;
  And so should you, to love things nothing worth.

NOTES: Continuing the theme from the previous sonnet, the poet advises against trying to defend him when he is gone, since the subject can do so only by giving the poet more credit than he is due. **Line 1,** *task you*: challenge or command you. **Line 4,** *you...nothing worthy prove*: you cannot show anything worthy in me. **Line 6,** *than mine own desert*: than I deserve. **Line 7,** *hang*: the allusion is to trophies or epitaphs hung in honor of heroes. **Line 8,** *niggard truth*: plain or unvarnished truth. **Line 9,** *true love*: honest affection. **Line 10,** *speak well of me untrue*: say complimentary but untruthful things about me. **Line 13,** *I am shamed...I bring forth*: I take no pride in my literary offerings. (Those who see Shakespeare speaking about himself in his sonnets often read this to be a confession of shame about his plays). **Line 14,** *things nothing worth*: such worthless things.

73

That time of year thou mayst in me behold
When yellow leaves, or none, or few, do hang
Upon those boughs which shake against the cold,
Bare ruined choirs, where late the sweet birds sang.
In me thou see'st the twilight of such day
As after sunset fadeth in the west,
Which, by and by, black night doth take away,
Death's second self, that seals up all in rest.
In me thou see'st the glowing of such fire
That on the ashes of his youth doth lie,
As the death-bed, whereon it must expire,
Consumed with that which it was nourished by.
  This thou perceivest, which makes thy love more strong,
  To love that well which thou must leave ere long.

NOTES: The poet, confronting the end of his life, finds his affection for the subject growing as death draws nears. **Lines 1-4,** *time of year:* the image suggests a man in the late fall or winter of his life. **Line 4,** *Bare ruined choirs:* the image appears to suggest the roofless choir loft of an old church or abbey in ruins. **Line 8,** *seals up:* ends or concludes. **Line 14,** *leave:* part with, or depart from.

74

But be contented when that fell arrest
Without all bail shall carry me away.
My life hath in this line some interest,
Which, for memorial, still with thee shall stay.
When thou reviewest this, thou dost review
The very part was consecrate to thee.
The earth can have but earth, which is his due;
My spirit is thine, the better part of me.
So then, thou hast but lost the dregs of life,
The prey of worms, my body being dead,
The coward conquest of a wretch's knife,
Too base of thee to be rememberèd.
  The worth of that is that which it contains;
  And that is this, and this with thee remains.

NOTES: Concluding the theme from the previous sonnet, the poet reassures the subject that while the poet's body may die, his spirit will live on in his poetry. **Line 1,** *fell arrest*: ie, Death. **Line 3,** *in this line*: in this verse. **Line 4,** *for memorial*: as a memento or reminder. **Line 5,** *reviewest*: re-read. **Lines 13-14***, The worth of that...with thee remains:* my real worth is in my spirit, which my body contains, and my spirit is embodied in this verse, which remains with you.

75

So are you to my thoughts as food to life,
Or as sweet-seasoned showers are to the ground.
And for the peace of you I hold such strife
As 'twixt a miser and his wealth is found.
Now proud as an enjoyer, and anon
Doubting the filching age will steal his treasure;
Now counting best to be with you alone,
Then bettered that the world may see my pleasure.
Sometime all full with feasting on your sight,
And, by and by, clean starvèd for a look;
Possessing or pursuing no delight,
Save what is had, or must from you be took.
   Thus do I pine and surfeit day by day,
   Or gluttoning on all, or all away.

NOTES: Likening himself to a greedy miser, the poet bemoans the miser's paradox: the inability to enjoy his wealth—ie, the subject's affection—for fear that he will lose it. (The sonnet also contains several bawdy puns, apparent to those who look carefully). **Line 2,** *sweet-seasoned showers*: Spring showers. **Line 3,** *peace of you*: the tranquility or contentment of your affection. (The line is also an apparent pun on "piece"—both to the portion of the subject's affection he holds, and its worth as a piece of treasure); *hold such strife*: suffer such conflict. **Line 6,** *doubting*: fearing; *the filching age*: these corrupt times. **Line 8,** *bettered*: made better. **Line 10,** *clean*: completely, utterly. **Line 13:** *pine*: starve; *surfeit*: glut or satiate.

76

Why is my verse so barren of new pride,
So far from variation or quick change?
Why with the time do I not glance aside
To new-found methods, and to compounds strange?
Why write I still all one, ever the same,
And keep invention in a noted weed,
That every word doth almost tell my name,
Showing their birth, and where they did proceed?
O know, sweet love, I always write of you,
And you and love are still my argument.
So all my best is dressing old words new,
Spending again what is already spent.
  For as the sun is daily new and old,
  So is my love still telling what is told.

NOTES: The poet remarks that the reason his poetry never seems to change is
that his subject is unchanging. **Line 1,** *new pride:* something new. **Line 3,** *with the
time:* ie, in accorandance with the latest fashion. **Line 4,** *compounds:* compound
words. **Line 6,** *invention:* creativity; *noted weed:* familiar clothing. **Line 10,** *still my
argument:* ever my theme or subject. **Line 11,** *all my best:* my best efforts; *dressing old
words new:* finding new ways of saying the same things.

77

Thy glass will show thee how thy beauties wear,
Thy dial how thy precious minutes waste.
The vacant leaves thy mind's imprint will bear,
And of this book, this learning mayst thou taste.
The wrinkles, which thy glass will truly show,
Of mouthèd graves will give thee memory.
Thou, by thy dial's shady stealth, mayst know
Time's thievish progress to eternity.
Look what thy memory can not contain;
Commit to these waste blanks, and thou shalt find
Those children nursed, delivered from thy brain,
To take a new acquaintance of thy mind.
   These offices, so oft as thou wilt look,
   Shall profit thee, and much enrich thy book.

NOTES: The topic of this sonnet was a blank notebook, sent as a gift, on which
it was supposed that the recipient would record thoughts and impressions. **Line
1,** *glass:* mirror; *wear:* endure, or hold up. **Line 2,** *dial:* sundial; *waste:* pass. **Line 3,**
vacant leaves: empty pages. **Line 6,** *mouthèd:* open, gaping. **Line 7,** *shady stealth:* ie, the
sundial's shadow as it moves with the sun. **Line 9,** *Look what:* whatever. **Line 10,**
waste blanks: empty pages. **Lines 11-12,** *Those children...of they brain:* your ideas,
recorded on these pages, will someday seem new to you. **Line 13,** *offices:* tasks.

78

So oft have I invoked thee for my Muse,
And found such fair assistance in my verse
As every alien pen hath got my use,
And under thee their poesy disperse.
Thine eyes, that taught the dumb on high to sing
And heavy ignorance aloft to fly,
Have added feathers to the learnèd's wing
And given grace a double majesty.
Yet, be most proud of that which I compile,
Whose influence is thine and born of thee.
In others' works thou dost but mend the style,
And arts with thy sweet graces gracèd be,
  But thou art all my art and dost advance
  As high as learning my rude ignorance.

NOTES: Despairing of his own talents, the poet remarks that others have taken to praising the subject in ways far better than he—although unlike the others, he owes whatever gifts he may have to the subject. **Line 1,** *for*: as. **Line 2,** *fair assistance*: kind or generous help. **Line 3,** *As*: that; *every alien pen hath got my use*: every other poet has taken up my habit (ie, of writing poems about the subject). **Line 4,** *under thee*: under your auspices or protection. (This line suggests that the subject may have been a patron of the arts). **Line 5,** *dumb*: mute; *on high to sing*: to sing loudly. **Line 6,** *heavy*: sluggish. **Line 7,** *added feathers*:: falconers would often add feathers to improve their birds' flight; the line suggests a similar effect the subject has on the learned. **Line 9,** *compile*: compose.

79

Whilst I alone did call upon thy aid,
My verse alone had all thy gentle grace.
But now, my gracious numbers are decayed,
And my sick Muse doth give another place.
I grant, sweet love, thy lovely argument
Deserves the travail of a worthier pen.
Yet, what of thee thy poet doth invent,
He robs thee of, and pays it thee again.
He lends thee virtue, and he stole that word
From thy behavior; beauty doth he give
And found it in thy cheek; he can afford
No praise to thee but what in thee doth live.
   Then thank him not for that which he doth say,
   Since what he owes thee, thou thyself dost pay.

NOTES: Continuing the topic of the previous sonnet, the poet complains that the other, worthier writers taking his place are only stealing their inspiration from the subject. **Line 1,** *call upon they aid*: invoke you as my Muse (or, for the cynics among us, enjoy your patronage). **Line 3,** *decayed*: of lesser quality. **Line 4,** *give another place*: make way for someone else. **Line 5,** *thy lovely argument*: the subject of your beauty. **Line 6,** *of thee*: about you; *invent*: compose. **Line 9,** *lends thee virtue*: credits or praises your virtue. **Line 11,** *afford*: give.

80

O, how I faint when I of you do write,
Knowing a better spirit doth use your name,
And in the praise thereof spends all his might
To make me tongue-tied, speaking of your fame.
But since your worth, wide as the ocean is,
The humble as the proudest sail doth bear,
My saucy bark, inferior far to his,
On your broad main doth wilfully appear.
Your shallowest help will hold me up afloat,
Whilst he upon your soundless deep doth ride.
Or, being wrecked, I am a worthless boat,
He of tall building, and of goodly pride.
   Then if he thrive, and I be cast away,
   The worst was this: my love was my decay.

NOTES: The poet compares his meager verses to a small boat that has difficulties sailing the same literary sea as the proud ship of his poetic rival. **Line 1,** *faint*: lose heart or courage. **Line 2,** *a better spirit*: a greater poet. **Line 6,** *The humble as the proudest sail*: a small boat as well as a mighty ship. **Line 7,** *my saucy bark*: my small (or impertinent) ship.. **Line 8,** *broad main*: wide or boundless ocean. **Line 10,** *soundless deep*: ocean depths too deep to be measured. **Line 11,** *boat*: a little ship. **Line 12,** *tall building*: grand construction. **Line 14,** *my decay*: the cause of his ruin.

81

Or I shall live your epitaph to make,
Or you survive when I in earth am rotten;
From hence, your memory death cannot take,
Although in me each part will be forgotten.
Your name from hence immortal life shall have,
Though I, once gone, to all the world must die.
The earth can yield me but a common grave,
When you entombèd in men's eyes shall lie.
Your monument shall be my gentle verse,
Which eyes not yet created shall o'er-read,
And tongues to be your being shall rehearse
When all the breathers of this world are dead.
   You still shall live–such virtue hath my pen–
   Where breath most breathes, even in the mouths of men.

NOTES: Returning to the them of poetic immortality, the poet suggests that while he himself will be completely forgotten, the subject will always be remembered because of the verse. (Of course, the assurances of Line 5 notwithstanding, while taking credit for the poem the poet never actually mentions the subject by name). **Line 1,** *Or*: either. **Line 4,** *in me each part*: all parts of me. **Line 7,** *common*: ordinary. **Line 8,** *entombèd in men's eyes*: buried in a place of prominence; or, anticipating the next line, memorialized where people will still see you. **Line 11,** *rehearse*: recite. **Line 13,** *such virtue has my pen*: so immortal are my poems. (So much for the despairing modesty of the preceeding two sonnets). **Line 14:** *breath...mouths of men*: this line plays upon the breath that is respiration, and the breath that articulates the words of the poem.

82

I grant thou wert not married to my Muse,
And therefore mayst without attaint o'erlook
The dedicated words which writers use
Of their fair subject, blessing every book.
Thou art as fair in knowledge as in hue,
Finding thy worth a limit past my praise,
And therefore art enforced to seek anew
Some fresher stamp of the time-bettering days.
And do so, love; yet when they have devised
What strainèd touches rhetoric can lend,
Thou, truly fair, wert truly sympathized
In true plain words by thy true-telling friend.
   And their gross painting might be better used
   Where cheeks need blood; in thee, it is abused.

NOTES: Here, the poet compares his own heartfelt verses to the exaggerated lines of others. **Line 1,** *married*: bound. **Line 2,** *attaint*: shame; *o'erlook*: read. **Line 3,** *dedicated words*: words of dedication, as in a book. **Line 8,** *stamp*: something that makes an impression, eg, an embossing stamp. **Line 11,** *sympathized*: expressed emotionally. **Line 12,** *plain*: honest or unadorned. **Lines 13-14,** *their gross painting...it is abused*: they might better use their artistic exaggerations on subjects that need it, rather than overdoing it on you.

83

I never saw that you did painting need,
And therefore to your fair no painting set.
I found, or thought I found, you did exceed
The barren tender of a poet's debt.
And, therefore, have I slept in your report,
That you yourself being extant well might show
How far a modern quill doth come too short,
Speaking of worth, what worth in you doth grow.
This silence for my sin you did impute,
Which shall be most my glory, being dumb,
For I impair not beauty being mute,
When others would give life, and bring a tomb.
   There lives more life in one of your fair eyes
   Than both your poets can, in praise, devise.

NOTES: The poet tries to atone for the being insufficiently effusive in lauding the subject by arguing that mere words cannot express sufficient praise. **Line 1,** *painting:* as in other sonnets, "painting" is used in the sense of false beauty or cosmetics. **Line 2,** *fair:* loveliness or beauty. Lines 3-, *you did exceed..a poet's debt:* your worthiness extends beyond the capacity of a worthless poem to recount. **Line 6,** *extant:* alive. **Line 7,** *a modern quill:* a small pen. **Line 8,** *worth:* value. **Line 9,** *impute:* deem, or consider. **Line 10,** *being dumb:* remaining silent. **Lines 11-12,** *For I impair not...bring a tomb:* while my silence does not diminish your beauty, other artists destroy it even as they try to bring it to life. **Line 14:** *both your poets:* this line suggests that the subject was patron to two rival poets.

84

Who is it that says most, which can say more
Than this rich praise, that you alone are you?
In whose confine immurèd is the store
Which should example where your equal grew?
Lean penury within that pen doth dwell
That to his subject lends not some small glory.
But he that writes of you, if he can tell
That you are you, so dignifies his story.
Let him but copy what in you is writ,
Not making worse what nature made so clear,
And such a counterpart shall fame his wit,
Making his style admired every where.
  You to your beauteous blessings add a curse:
  Being fond on praise, which makes your praises worse.

NOTES: The poet chastises the subject for caring too much for insincere praise, since true praise consists of reflecting the subject's perfections, rather than exaggerating them. **Lines 3-4,** *In whose confine...where your equal grew*: you contain all beauty, from which comparisons will be made. **Line 8,** *so*: thus, in this way; *dignifies his story*: elevates his writing. **Line 9,** *copy*: transcribe. **Line 11,** *fame*: make famous. **Line 14,** *Being fond on praise*: eagerly seeking or encouraging praise.

85

My tongue-tied Muse in manners holds her still,
While comments of your praise, richly compiled,
Reserve their character with golden quill
And precious phrase by all the Muses filed.
I think good thoughts, whilst other write good words,
And like unlettered clerk still cry "Amen"
To every hymn that able spirit affords
In polished form of well-refinèd pen.
Hearing you praised, I say "'Tis so, 'tis true,"
And, to the most of praise, add something more.
But that is in my thought, whose love to you,
Though words come hindmost, holds his rank before.
  Then others for the breath of words respect,
  Me for my dumb thoughts, speaking in effect.

NOTES: While others praise the subject effusively, the poet explains that he agrees
with the sentiments of others, but adds something that they lack: his love. **Line 1,**
in manners holds her still: stays quiet out of politeness. **Line 2,** *comments of your praise*:
things written praising you. **Line 3,** *Reserve their character*: preserve this literary style.
Line 4, *filed*: polished or smoothed. **Line 5,** *other*: others. **Line 6,** *unlettered clerk*: an
illiterate assistant who utters to prayers led by the "lettered" parson. **Line 10,** *most*:
utmost. **Line 12,** *holds his rank before*: keeps it (ie, my thoughts of love) foremost.
Lines 13-14, *others for the breath...speaking in effect*: others take notice of expressions
of praise (even though it may be mere breath—or "hot air"), while I regard my
unspoken thoughts of love as the real truth.

86

Was it the proud full sail of his great verse,
Bound for the prize of all-too-precious you,
That did my ripe thoughts in my brain inhearse,
Making their tomb the womb wherein they grew?
Was it his spirit, by spirits taught to write
Above a mortal pitch, that struck me dead?
No; neither he, nor his compeers by night
Giving him aid, my verse astonishèd.
He, nor that affable familiar ghost
Which nightly gulls him with intelligence,
As victors of my silence cannot boast.
I was not sick of any fear from thence.
  But when your countenance filled up his line,
  Then lacked I matter; that enfeebled mine.

NOTES: Recalling the nautical imagery of a previous sonnet, and noting that his poetic rival appears to have won the subject's favor, the poet observes that this leaves him with little to write about. **Line 1,** *proud full:* stately, (with a wordplay on prideful). **Line 2,** *Bound for the prize:* the image suggests a pirate sailing off in search of treasure. (These were, after all, the days of Sir Francis Drake). **Line 3,** *inhearse:* entomb. **Line 5,** *spirit:* mental energy. **Line 6,** *pitch:* attainment. (In falconry, the bird's pitch is its highest point of flight before swooping down after its prey). **Line 7,** *compeers:* companions, or fellow students. **Line 8,** *astonishèd:* stunned. **Line 9,** *He, nor:* neither he nor; *ghost:* spirit (perchance, not the sort that jumpeth out and crieth "Boo!"). **Line 10,** *gulls:* cheats; *intelligence:* news. **Line 13,** *countenance:* face, or patronage. **Line 14:** *lacked I matter:* I had no subject (to write about).

87

Farewell! Thou art too dear for my possessing,
And like enough thou know'st thy estimate.
The charter of thy worth gives thee releasing;
My bonds in thee are all determinate.
For how do I hold thee but by thy granting,
And for that riches where is my deserving?
The cause of this fair gift in me is wanting,
And so my patent back again is swerving.
Thyself thou gavest, thy own worth then not knowing,
Or me, to whom thou gavest it, else mistaking;
So thy great gift, upon misprision growing,
Comes home again, on better judgment making.
   Thus have I had thee, as a dream doth flatter—
   In sleep a king, but waking no such matter.

NOTES: In this sonnet, the poet laments the ending of his relationship with the subject; the overtones in many of the lines (eg, how do I hold thee...have I had thee..thyself thou gavest, etc.) imply that the relationship may have been a romantic one. Like Sonnet 20, this poem is noteworthy for its use of "feminine" rhymes. **Line 1,** *dear*: precious, (or expensive). **Line 2,** *like enough*: probably; *estimate*: value. **Line 3,** *charter*: entitlement. (A charter was an official document granting its possessor legal rights and privileges); *gives thee releasing*: sets you free. **Line 4,** *my bonds in thee*: claims to you; *determinate*: at an end, over. **Line 8,** *patent*: privilege or right. **Line 10,** *Or me...else mistaking*: or else you mistook my own worth, when you gave yourself to me. **Line 11,** *misprison*: misunderstanding. **Line 12,** *on better judgment making*: ie, on second thought; or on coming to your senses.

88

When thou shalt be disposed to set me light,
And place my merit in the eye of scorn,
Upon thy side against myself I'll fight
And prove thee virtuous, though thou art forsworn.
With mine own weakness being best acquainted,
Upon thy part I can set down a story
Of faults concealed, wherein I am attainted,
That thou, in losing me, shalt win much glory.
And I, by this, will be a gainer too,
For bending all my loving thoughts on thee,
The injuries that to myself I do,
Doing thee vantage, double-vantage me.
  Such is my love, to thee I so belong,
    That for thy right, myself will bear all wrong.

NOTES: The poet suggest that by dishonoring himself, and taking the subject's side of whatever has come between them, it will make the subject look better—which, in the end, is all the poet wants. **Line 1,** *set me light*: treat or regard me lightly. **Line 2,** *place my merit in the eye of scorn*: hold me up to ridicule. **Line 6,** *Upon they part*: taking your side. **Line 7,** *attained*: dishonored. **Line 8,** *losing*: destroying. **Line 12,** *vantage*: benefit; *double-vantage*: doubly benefit. **Line 14,** *for thy right*: on your behalf.

89

Say that thou didst forsake me for some fault,
And I will comment upon that offence.
Speak of my lameness, and I straight will halt,
Against thy reasons making no defense.
Thou canst not, love, disgrace me half so ill,
To set a form upon desired change,
As I'll myself disgrace; knowing thy will,
I will acquaintance strangle and look strange,
Be absent from thy walks, and in my tongue
Thy sweet belovèd name no more shall dwell,
Lest I, too much profane, should do it wrong,
And haply of our old acquaintance tell.
  For thee against myself I'll vow debate,
  For I must ne'er love him whom thou dost hate.

NOTES: Continuing the theme from the previous sonnet, the poet suggests ways
that he will honor his estranged beloved by supporting anything said against
himself. **Line 1,** *Say*: announce. **Line 3,** *straight will halt*: will limp at once. **Line 4,**
reasons: statements or assertions. **Line 5,** *ill*: badly. **Line 6,** *To set a form upon*: to give
order to. **Line 8,** *I will acquaintance...look strange*: I will suppress the fact of our
acquaintance and behave as if we were strangers. **Line 9,** *thy walks*: the places you
frequent. **Line 11,** *profane*: impious. **Line 12,** *haply*: perhaps. **Line 13,** *For thee*: on
your behalf; *debate*: combat.

90

Then hate me when thou wilt; if ever, now.
Now, while the world is bent my deeds to cross,
Join with the spite of fortune, make me bow,
And do not drop in for an afterloss.
Ah, do not, when my heart hath 'scaped this sorrow,
Come in the rearward of a conquered woe.
Give not a windy night a rainy morrow,
To linger out a purposed overthrow.
If thou wilt leave me, do not leave me last,
When other petty griefs have done their spite,
But in the onset come, so shall I taste
At first the very worst of fortune's might.
   And other strains of woe, which now seem woe,
   Compared with loss of thee will not seem so.

NOTES: Building upon the thought from the previous sonnet, the poet asks the subject to deliver whatever blows await now, since anything the world can inflict will seem light in comparison. **Line 1,** *Then*: therefore. **Line 2,** *bent my deeds to cross*: determined to thwart whatever I do. **Line 4,** *bow*: submit. **Line 4,** *afterloss*: subsequent misfortune. **Line 5,** *'scaped this sorrow*: recovered from these present woes. **Line 6,** *a conquered woe*: a sorrow overcome. **Line 8,** *linger out*: stretch out or lengthen; *overthrow*: defeat. **Line 11,** *in the onset*: in the beginning (ie, in an initial wave of a military attack). **Line 13,** *strains*: types or kinds.

91

Some glory in their birth, some in their skill,
Some in their wealth, some in their bodies' force,
Some in their garments, though new-fangled ill,
Some in their hawks and hounds, some in their horse.
And every humor hath his adjunct pleasure,
Wherein it finds a joy above the rest.
But these particulars are not my measure,
All these I better in one general best.
Thy love is better than high birth to me,
Richer than wealth, prouder than garments' cost,
Of more delight than hawks or horses be.
And having thee, of all men's pride I boast,
    Wretched in this alone: that thou mayst take
    All this away, and me most wretched make.

NOTES: Comparing the subject's love to other sources of pride and honor, the poet frets losing that love would make him miserable. **Line 1,** *birth*: lineage; *skill*: artistry or cleverness. **Line 2,** *force*: strength. **Line 3,** *new-fangled ill*: the ugly fashion of the day. **Line 5,** *humor*: temperament; *adjunct*: accompanying. **Line 7,** *my measure*: my standard. **Line 10,** *prouder*: finer, more spendid. **Line 12,** *all men's pride*: all treasures that men may possess.

92

But do thy worst to steal thyself away,
For term of life thou art assurèd mine,
And life no longer than thy love will stay,
For it depends upon that love of thine.
Then need I not to fear the worst of wrongs,
When in the least of them my life hath end.
I see a better state to me belongs
Than that which on thy humor doth depend.
Thou canst not vex me with inconstant mind,
Since that my life on thy revolt doth lie.
O, what a happy title do I find,
Happy to have thy love, happy to die!
   But what's so blessèd-fair that fears no blot?
   Thou mayst be false, and yet I know it not.

NOTES: Following the thought that closes the previous sonnet, the poet reflects that he really need not fear the loss of the subject's love: since the loss would kill him anyway, at least he would not be suffering. **Line 2,** *term of life*: a legal phrase, denoting the right of possession for the owner's lifetime; *assurèd*: pledged. (The line suggests a legally binding relationship, such as husband-wife, or a betrothal). **Line 3,** *stay*: remain. **Line 4,** *it*: ie, my life. **Line 8,** *humor*: whim or mood. **Lines 9-10,** *Thou canst not vex me...revolt doth lie*: ie, your inconstancy cannot really bother me, since it would kill me. (Lovers, it seems, were adept at finding silver linings in Elizabethan times). **Line 11,** *happy title*: fortunate right. **Line 13,** *blessèd-fair*: lucky and lovely.

93

So shall I live, supposing thou art true,
Like a deceivèd husband; so love's face
May still seem love to me, though altered new—
Thy looks with me, thy heart in other place.
For there can live no hatred in thine eye,
Therefore in that I cannot know thy change.
In many's looks the false heart's history
Is writ in moods and frowns and wrinkles strange.
But Heaven in thy creation did decree
That in thy face sweet love should ever dwell;
Whate'er thy thoughts or thy heart's workings be,
Thy looks should nothing thence but sweetness tell.
   How like Eve's apple doth thy beauty grow,
   If thy sweet virtue answer not thy show!

NOTES: Continuing the concluding thought of the preceding sonnet, the poet remarks that the subject's supreme loveliness may mask a falseness that he would be powerless to detect. **Line 1,** *So*: therefore; *supposing*: believing. **Line 3,** *still*: continue to; *though altered new*: even if it has changed. **Line 4,** *looks*: affectionate glances, or outward appearance; *heart*: affections. **Line 5,** *in thine eye*: in your appearance or bearing. **Line 7,** *looks*: facial expressions. **Line 12:** *looks*: appearance. **Line 14,** *answer not*: is inconsistent with.

94

They that have power to hurt and will do none,
That do not do the thing they most do show,
Who, moving others, are themselves as stone,
Unmovèd, cold, and to temptation slow—
They rightly do inherit heaven's graces
And husband nature's riches from expense.
They are the lords and owners of their faces,
Others but stewards of their excellence.
The summer's flower is to the summer sweet,
Though to itself it only live and die;
But if that flower with base infection meet,
The basest weed outbraves his dignity.
    For sweetest things turn sourest by their deeds;
    Lilies that fester smell far worse than weeds.

NOTES: The poet contrasts different types of people blessed by circum-
stance—those who use their good fortune to try to better the world, and those
who are corrupted by their gifts. **Line 2,** *the thing..do show*: what appearances suggest
they are likeliest to do. **Line 4,** *to temptation slow*: not easily prone to temptation.
Line 5, *Heaven's graces*: good fortune (ie, the "grace of God"). **Line 6,** *husband*:
protect; *expense*: waste. **Line 7,** *faces*: appearances. **Line 8,** *stewards*: overseers. **Line
12,** *basest*: lowliest; *outbraves*: surpasses.

95

How sweet and lovely dost thou make the shame
Which, like a canker in the fragrant rose,
Doth spot the beauty of thy budding name!
O, in what sweets dost thou thy sins enclose!
That tongue that tells the story of thy days,
Making lascivious comments on thy sport,
Cannot dispraise but in a kind of praise;
Naming thy name blesses an ill report.
O, what a mansion have those vices got,
Which for their habitation chose out thee,
Where beauty's veil doth cover every blot,
And all things turns to fair that eyes can see!
 Take heed, dear heart, of this large privilege;
 The hardest knife ill-used doth lose his edge.

NOTES: In this sonnet, the poet warns against using beauty to mask a dishonorable core. **Line 1,** *shame*: disgraceful behavior. **Line 2,** *canker*: worm. **Lines 3,** *spot the beauty of thy budding name*: a cankerworm entering a rose will leave a small blemish in the immature bud, the damage becoming apparent when the blossom opens. **Line 4,** *sweets*: sweet-smelling fragrances. **Line 6,** *sport*: hijinks. (The "lascivious comments" did not involve the sport of basketball). **Line 8,** *ill report*: bad reputation. **Line 10,** *habitation*: abode, or custom. **Line 11,** *beauty's veil*: the obscuring effects of beauty. **Line 12,** *all things turns to fair that eyes can see*: ie, beauty's veil converts everything visible into loveliness. (Some editors read the line as "turn," but this changes the reference from "beauty's veil" to "all things," and obscures the suggestion that there may be things that eyes cannot see). **Line 13,** *privilege*: freedom or advantage.

96

Some say thy fault is youth, some wantonness,
Some say thy grace is youth and gentle sport.
Both grace and faults are loved of more and less;
Thou makest faults graces that to thee resort.
As on the finger of a thronèd queen
The basest jewel will be well esteemed,
So are those errors that in thee are seen
To truths translated, and for true things deemed.
How many lambs might the stern wolf betray
If like a lamb he could his looks translate;
How many gazers mightst thou lead away,
If thou wouldst use the strength of all thy state!
   But do not so; I love thee in such sort
   As, thou being mine, mine is thy good report.

NOTES: Continuing the theme of the previous sonnet. **Line 1,** *wantonness*: arrogance or promiscuity. **Line 2,** *grace*: charm; *gentle sport*: a polite way of saying wantonness (ie, the sporting endeavors mentioned in the previous sonnet). **Line 3,** *of more and less*: by those of high and low stations in life. **Line 4,** *makest faults...to thee resort*: turn your faults into graces. **Line 8,** *translated*: transformed. **Line 10,** *If like a lamb...translate*: if he (ie, the stern wolf) could make himself look like a lamb. **Line 12,** *the strength of all thy state*: all the powers at your command. **Lines 13-14:** here, the poet repeats the closing couplet of Sonnet 36 and, although the admonition is different., they appear as two sides of the same coin. In the earlier sonnet, the poet is commenting that the subject's honor reflects well on the poet; here, the poet frets that the subject's actions in leading others astray will reflect *badly* on the poet.

97

How like a winter hath my absence been
From thee, the pleasure of the fleeting year!
What freezings have I felt, what dark days seen!
What old December's bareness everywhere!
And yet, this time removed was summer's time,
The teeming autumn, big with rich increase,
Bearing the wanton burden of the prime,
Like widowed wombs after their lords' decease.
Yet this abundant issue seemed to me
But hope of orphans and unfathered fruit;
For summer and his pleasures wait on thee,
And thou away, the very birds are mute.
   Or, if they sing, 'tis with so dull a cheer
   That leaves look pale, dreading the winter's near.

NOTES: Here, the poet likens his absence from the subject to the bleakness of winter. **Line 5,** *this time removed*: ie, this time we have been apart. **Line 6,** *teeming*: fruitful, or pregnant. (The poem employs images of fertility throughout, in contrast to the barren days of winter). **Line 7,** *wanton burden of the prime*: luxuriant offspring of Spring. **Line 8,** *widowed wombs*: a womb bearing the child of the woman's deceased husband. **Line 9,** *abundant issue*: fruitful bounty. **Line 10,** *unfathered fruit*: (continuing the imagery) a posthumous—ie, fatherless—child. **Line 11,** *wait on thee*: serve and attend you. **Line 12,** *thou away*: you being gone. **Line 13,** *with so dull a cheer*: so faintheartedly.

98

From you have I been absent in the spring,
When proud-pièd April, dressed in all his trim,
Hath put a spirit of youth in every thing;
That heavy Saturn laughed and leaped with him.
Yet nor the lays of birds, nor the sweet smell
Of different flowers in odor and in hue
Could make me any summer's story tell,
Or from their proud lap pluck them where they grew.
Nor did I wonder at the lily's white,
Nor praise the deep vermilion in the rose.
They were but sweet, but figures of delight,
Drawn after you, you pattern of all those.
  Yet seemed it winter still; and, you away,
  As with your shadow I with these did play.

NOTES: Continuing the theme from the previous sonnet, the poet here suggests
that the subject's absence muted the beauty of springtime. **Line 2,** *proud-pièd April*:
April exulting in the vibrancy of color. **Line 4,** *Saturn*: to the superstitious, people
born under the influence of Planet Saturn were thought to be heavy and saturine—
ie, of sluggish or gloomy temperament. **Line 5,** *lays*: songs. **Line 6,** *different flowers*:
various or other flowers. **Line 8,** *their proud lap*: the teeming earth. **Line 11,** *but*:
merely. **Line 12,** *Drawn after*: copies of.

99

The forward violet thus did I chide:
Sweet thief, whence didst thou steal thy sweet that smells
If not from my love's breath? The purple pride,
Which on thy soft cheek for complexion dwells,
In my love's veins thou hast too grossly dyed.
The lily I condemnèd for thy hand,
And buds of marjoram had stol'n thy hair.
The roses fearfully on thorns did stand,
One blushing shame, another white despair;
A third, nor red nor white, had stol'n of both
And to his robbery had annexed thy breath;
But, for his theft, in pride of all his growth
A vengeful canker eat him up to death.
   More flowers I noted, yet I none could see
   But sweet or color it had stol'n from thee.

NOTES: This poem continues the theme from the previous sonnet...and yes, it does indeed have fifteen lines. (Apparently, poets in Elizabethan England paid as little attention to math as they do today: an extra line was added to the first quatrain. Either that, or he simply miscounted). **Line 1,** *forward*: cheeky or precocious (the violet is one of the earlier flowers to bloom in the spring). **Line 3,** *purple*: in Shakespeare's day, "purple" included colors ranging from violet to bright red. **Line 4,** *for complexion*: as a cosmetic. **Line 5,** *grossly*: excessively. **Line 6,** *The lily I condemnèd for thy hand*: I accused the white lily of stealing the fair complexion of your hand. **Line 8,** *on thorns*: ie, in a state of anxiety. **Line 15,** *But*: except.

100

Where art thou, Muse, that thou forget'st so long
To speak of that which gives thee all thy might?
Spend'st thou thy fury on some worthless song,
Darkening thy power to lend base subjects light?
Return, forgetful Muse, and straight redeem
In gentle numbers time so idly spent;
Sing to the ear that doth thy lays esteem
And gives thy pen both skill and argument.
Rise, resty Muse, my love's sweet face survey,
If time have any wrinkle graven there.
If any, be a satire to decay,
And make Time's spoils despisèd every where.
  Give my love fame faster than Time wastes life,
  So thou prevent'st his scythe and crooked knife.

NOTES: The poet returns to the theme of immortality through poetry and laments having neglected praising his subject for a time, blaming his Muse for neglecting his subject. **Line 3,** *fury*: passion or enthusiasm. **Line 4,** *lend base subjects light*: illuminate lowly subjects. **Line 6,** *gentle numbers*: noble or refined verses. **Line 7,** *lays*: songs or verses. **Line 8,** *argument*: subject or theme. **Line 9,** *resty*: tired or sluggish. **Line 11,** *be a satire to*: mock or satirize. **Line 13:** *wastes*: destroys.

101

O truant Muse, what shall be thy amends
For thy neglect of truth in beauty dyed?
Both truth and beauty on my love depends.
So dost thou too, and therein dignified.
Make answer, Muse: wilt thou not haply say
Truth needs no color, with his color fixed;
Beauty no pencil, beauty's truth to lay;
But best is best, if never intermixed?
Because he needs no praise, wilt thou be dumb?
Excuse not silence so, for't lies in thee
To make him much outlive a gilded tomb,
And to be praised of ages yet to be.
   Then do thy office, Muse; I teach thee how
   To make him seem long hence as he shows now.

NOTES: Continuing the theme from the previous sonnet, the poet demands that inspiration strike, noting that poetic immorality does, after all, need an actual poem in order to accomplish its purpose. **Line 1,** *truant*: wandering; *what shall be thy amends*: how will you atone? **Line 2,** *dyed*: steeped. **Line 4,** *dignified*: are you dignified. **Line 5,** *haply*: perhaps. **Line 6,** *Truth*: reality; *color*: artificial enhancement. **Line 7,** *lay*: depict. **Line 9,** *dumb*: mute. **Line 11,** *much*: long. **Line 12,** *of ages*: ie, by future generations. **Line 13,** *do thy office*: do your duty. **Line 14,** *make him seem...shows now*: portray him in the future as he is now (ie, in all his glory).

102

My love is strengthened, though more weak in seeming;
I love not less, though less the show appear.
That love is merchandized whose rich esteeming
The owner's tongue doth publish everywhere.
Our love was new, and then but in the spring,
When I was wont to greet it with my lays,
As Philomel in summer's front doth sing,
And stops her pipe in growth of riper days.
Not that the summer is less pleasant now
Than when her mournful hymns did hush the night,
But that wild music burdens every bough,
And sweets grown common lose their dear delight.
   Therefore, like her, I sometime hold my tongue,
   Because I would not dull you with my song.

NOTES: The poet tries to justify his lack of poetic inspiration by suggesting that
he does not want to bore the subject through constant praise. **Line 1,** *love:*
affection; *seeming:* appearance. **Line 2,** *show:* display. **Line 3,** *merchandized:* bought
and sold; commercialized. **Line 4,** *publish:* proclaim, or make known. **Line 5,** *in the*
spring: ie, just beginning. **Line 6,** *lays:* poems or songs. **Line 7,** *As Philomel in*
summer's front: like the nightingale in early summer. **Line 8,** *stops her pipe:* stops
singing. (Nightingales have never been heavy smokers). **Line 13,** *sometime:*
sometimes, occasionally. **Line 14,** *dull you:* bore you.

103

Alack, what poverty my Muse brings forth,
That, having such a scope to show her pride,
The argument all bare is of more worth
Than when it hath my added praise beside.
O, blame me not, if I no more can write!
Look in your glass, and there appears a face
That overgoes my blunt invention quite,
Dulling my lines and doing me disgrace.
Were it not sinful then, striving to mend,
To mar the subject that before was well?
For to no other pass my verses tend
Than of your graces, and your gifts to tell.
  And more, much more, than in my verse can sit
  Your own glass shows you, when you look in it.

NOTES: Still searching for an excuse for his poetic inaction, the poet suggests at last that since the subject's beauty far surpasses mere words, silence is perhaps the finest tribute. (We do not know how this suggestion was received, but it appears to be the final sonnet in the set). **Line 1,** *poverty*: poor material; *Muse*: poetic inspiration. **Line 2,** *to show her pride*: to demonstrate how good she is. **Line 3,** *argument all bare*: unadorned subject (an early version of "naked truth"). **Lines 6, 14,** *glass*: mirror. **Line 7,** *overgoes*: surpasses; *blunt invention*: clumsy attempts at being creative. **Line 8,** *Dulling...doing me disgrace*: shaming me by taking the shine out of my writing. **Line 11,** *pass*: end or subject.

104

To me, fair friend, you never can be old,
For as you were when first your eye I eyed,
Such seems your beauty still. Three winters cold
Have from the forests shook three summers' pride.
Three beauteous springs to yellow autumn turned
In process of the seasons have I seen.
Three April perfumes in three hot Junes burned,
Since first I saw you fresh, which yet are green.
Ah! yet doth beauty, like a dial hand,
Steal from his figure and no pace perceived;
So your sweet hue, which methinks still doth stand,
Hath motion, and mine eye may be deceived.
  For fear of which, hear this, thou age unbred:
  Ere you were born was beauty's summer dead.

NOTES: Remarking upon one's inability to perceive small changes as they occur around us, the poet reflects that the subject's beauty is altering as well, though he cannot perceive it—and worries that the future will not know such beauty, once the subject passes from the world. **Line 2,** *when first your eye I eyed*: when I saw you for the first time. **Lines 3-8,** *Three winter's cold...*: The sonnet seems to recount a friendship that has lasted three years. **Line 4,** *pride*: splendor. **Line 9,** *like a dial hand...and no pace perceived*: like a shadow moving imperceptibly over a sundial. **Line 11,** *hue*: appearance; *still doth stand*: remains unchanged. **Line 13,** *age unbred*: future era. **Line 14,** *beauty's summer*: the peak of beauty.

105

Let not my love be called idolatry,
Nor my belovèd as an idol show,
Since all alike my songs and praises be
To one, of one, still such, and ever so.
Kind is my love today, tomorrow kind,
Still constant in a wondrous excellence;
Therefore my verse to constancy confined,
One thing expressing, leaves out difference.
"Fair, kind, and true" is all my argument;
"Fair, kind, and true" varying to other words.
And in this change is my invention spent,
Three themes in one, which wondrous scope affords.
   "Fair, kind, and true," have often lived alone,
   Which three, till now, never kept seat in one.

NOTES: The poet plays with conventional notions of "idolatry"—ie, the pagan or polytheistic worship of idols or false gods—by making an argument in justification of his worship of the subject along traditional theological lines: posturing a "holy trinity" of worth in his one "true" love. **Line 2,** *show*: appear. **Line 8,** *difference*: distinctions. **Line 9,** *argument*: subject. **Line 11,** *change*: variety or distinction.

106

When in the chronicle of wasted time
I see descriptions of the fairest wights,
And beauty making beautiful old rhyme
In praise of ladies dead and lovely knights,
Then, in the blazon of sweet beauty's best,
Of hand, of foot, of lip, of eye, of brow,
I see their antique pen would have expressed
Even such a beauty as you master now.
So all their praises are but prophecies
Of this our time, all you prefiguring;
And, for they looked but with divining eyes,
They had not still enough your worth to sing.
   For we, which now behold these present days,
   Had eyes to wonder, but lack tongues to praise.

NOTES: The poet suggests that all the poets of the past might have been worthier recounters of the subject's beauty than the lesser poets of the present, but lacked the subject matter. **Line 1,** *wasted time*: bygone days; time passed and gone. **Line 2,** *wights*: persons. (The term was archaic even in Shakespeare's day, suggesting a conscious affectation). **Line 5,** *blazon*: conspicuous display (*lit*, a coat of arms). **Line 8,** *master*: possess. **Line 10,** *prefiguring*: foreshadowing. **Line 11,** *for*: but for that; *divining*: foreseeing. **Line 12,** *still*: as yet. (Most editors alter the original to read "skill," but this seems to alter the meaning of the text). **Line 14,** *Had eye...tongues to praises*: we can look on with amazement, but lack the language skills needed to due the subject justice.

107

Not mine own fears, nor the prophetic soul
Of the wide world, dreaming on things to come,
Can yet the lease of my true love control,
Supposed as forfeit to a cónfined doom.
The mortal moon hath her eclipse endured,
And the sad augurs mock their own presage.
Incertainties now crown themselves assured,
And peace proclaims olives of endless age.
Now, with the drops of this most balmy time,
My love looks fresh, and death to me subscribes,
Since, spite of him, I'll live in this poor rhyme
While he insults o'er dull and speechless tribes.
   And thou in this shalt find thy monument,
   When tyrants' crests and tombs of brass are spent.

NOTES: The apparent catastrophe that forms the basis for this sonnet is a source of controversy. Perhaps the likeliest is the death of Queen Elizabeth in 1603; others include earlier illnesses by the Queen, her advancing old age, and the Spanish Armada. **Line 3,** *lease:* term or duration. **Line 4:** *Supposed as forfeit to a cónfined doom:* thought doomed to restrictions. **Line 5,** *mortal moon:* Queen Elizabeth, who died on March 24, 1603. (This reference, probably the key to unraveling the controversy, is as murky today as ever). **Line 6,** *sad augurs:* prophets of disaster; *presage:* predictions or warnings. **Line 7,** *Incertainties:* uncertainties. **Line 8,** *olives:* the olive branch is a symbol of peace. **Lines 7-8,** the "incertainties" that have been "assured" and brought the "olives" of peace may refer to the non-violent ascension of King James to the throne. **Line 10,** *subscribes:* yields. **Line 12,** *insults:* triumphs or prevails; *speechless:* illiterate. **Line 14,** *spent:* wasted away.

108

What's in the brain that ink may character
Which hath not figured to thee my true spirit?
What's new to speak, what now to register,
That may express my love or thy dear merit?
Nothing, sweet boy; but yet, like prayers divine,
I must each day say o'er the very same,
Counting no old thing old, thou mine, I thine,
Even as when first I hallowed thy fair name.
So that eternal love in love's fresh case
Weighs not the dust and injury of age,
Nor gives to necessary wrinkles place,
But makes antiquity for aye his page,
    Finding the first conceit of love there bred
    Where time and outward form would show it dead.

NOTES: The poet likens his expressions of love to daily prayers—which are also repeated often. **Line 1,** *character*: write. **Line 2,** *figured*: portrayed. **Line 3,** *register*: record. **Line 7,** *counting*: deeming. **Line 8,** *hallowed*: deemed holy. (One might wonder whether the Spanish Inquisition would have taken a less-hallowed view of secularizing the Lord's Prayer). **Line 10,** *Weighs not*: does not notice. **Line 11,** *place*: status or importance. **Line 12,** *antiquity*: old age; *page*: a young male servant. **Line 13,** *conceit*: idea or thought. **Line 14,** *show it*: would make it appear to be.

109

O, never say that I was false of heart,
Though absence seemed my flame to qualify.
As easy might I from myself depart
As from my soul, which in thy breast doth lie.
That is my home of love; if I have ranged,
Like him that travels I return again,
Just to the time, not with the time exchanged,
So that myself bring water for my stain.
Never believe, though in my nature reigned
All frailties that besiege all kinds of blood,
That it could so preposterously be stained
To leave for nothing all thy sum of good.
   For nothing this wide universe I call,
   Save thou, my rose; in it thou art my all.

NOTES: Acknowledging that he may have strayed, the poet insists that his return to fidelity, however fleeting, washes away any problems. **Line 2,** *flame*: passion; *qualify*: moderate or abate. **Line 5,** *ranged*: strayed or wandered. **Line 7,** *Just to the time...time exchanged*: exactly as before, notwithstanding anything I may have done in the interval. **Line 8,** *myself bring water for my stain*: the line evokes the idea, consistent with Christian theology, that water can cleanse sin. (As one authority notes, the illogic of this line lends wit to the verse even as it destroys the poet's premise—that his return cancels the crime of his departure...for though "water can wash away a stain...the periodic returns of a promiscuous lover do not wash away the crime of his infidelities." Booth, *Shakespeare's Sonnets*, p 352). **Line 10,** *all kinds of blood*: every sort of temperament. **Line 11,** *preposterously*: absurdly or unnaturally. **Line 12,** *for nothing*: for something worthless. **Line 14,** *rose*: Shakespeare often uses the rose as a symbol of perfect beauty.

110

Alas, 'tis true I have gone here and there
And made myself a motley to the view,
Gored mine own thoughts, sold cheap what is most dear,
Made old offences of affections new.
Most true it is that I have looked on truth
Askance and strangely; but, by all above,
These blenches gave my heart another youth,
And worse essays proved thee my best of love.
Now all is done, have what shall have no end.
Mine appetite I never more will grind
On newer proof, to try an older friend,
A god in love, to whom I am confined.
    Then give me welcome, next my heaven the best,
    Even to thy pure and most most loving breast.

NOTES: Continuing the theme of his own infidelity, the poet now insists that his wanderings have only given new life to his love for the subject. (This brash and witty train of logic probably worked no better in Shakespeare's day than it does now). **Line 2,** *motley*: jester; *made myself a motley to the view*: made a public fool of myself. **Line 3,** *Gored*: wounded. **Line 4,** *Made old offenses of affections new*: awakened the usual resentments by my new dalliances. **Line 5,** *truth*: honesty or faithfulness. **Line 6,** *Askance and strangely*: disdainfully and coldly. **Line 7,** *blenches*: sideways glances, or deviations; *gave my heart another youth*: rejuvenated my heart. **Line 8,** *worse essays*: less worthy experiments. **Line 9,** *have what shall have no end*: ie, take what will always be. **Lines 10-11,** *Mine appetite...on newer proof*: I will no longer satisfy myself with my experiments (ie, the carnal essays of Line 8). **Line 11,** *try*: afflict or test. **Line 12,** *confined*: limited. **Line 13,** *next my heaven the best*: the next best thing to heaven. **Line 14,** *most most loving*: very most loving; or most promiscuous.

111

O, for my sake do you with Fortune chide,
The guilty goddess of my harmful deeds,
That did not better for my life provide
Than public means, which public manners breeds.
Thence comes it that my name receives a brand,
And almost thence my nature is subdued
To what it works in, like the dyer's hand.
Pity me then, and wish I were renewed,
Whilst, like a willing patient, I will drink
Potions of eisel 'gainst my strong infection;
No bitterness that I will bitter think,
Nor double penance, to correct correction.
   Pity me then, dear friend, and I assure ye,
   Even that your pity is enough to cure me.

NOTES: The poet acknowledges that his highly public profession (which, in Shakespeare's case, was well known) places him in a position where his own bad behavior is both encouraged and brought to public scrutiny. (Along with the various "Will" sonnets, it tends to refute those who doubt that Shakespeare wrote his own material). **Line 2,** *The guilty goddess of*: the goddess who is responsible for. **Line 3-4,** *That did not better...which public manners breeds*: that did not provide a loftier way of life than living on public acclaim. (The term "public manners" also conveys a sense of ostentatious displays and easy familiarity, which the poet is blaming for whatever misdeeds he has committed). **Line 5,** *a brand*: a mark of shame. (In Shakespeare's day, criminals were sometimes branded on their foreheads). **Line 8,** *renewed*: revived. **Line 10,** *eisel*: vinegar; *strong infection*: ie, the plague. (Vinegar was often used as part of a medicinal potion to fight the plague). **Line 11,** *No bitterness*: ie, there is no bitter-tasting medicine *bitter*: acrid (ie, bitter). **Line 14,** *Even that your pity*: your pity alone.

112

Your love and pity doth the impression fill,
Which vulgar scandal stamped upon my brow.
For what care I who calls me well or ill,
So you o'er-green my bad, my good allow?
You are my all the world, and I must strive
To know my shames and praises from your tongue,
None else to me, nor I to none alive,
That my steeled sense or changes right or wrong.
In so profound abysm I throw all care
Of others' voices, that my adder's sense
To critic and to flatterer stoppèd are.
Mark how with my neglect I do dispense—
   You are so strongly in my purpose bred
   That all the world besides methinks are dead.

NOTES: Continuing the theme from the previous sonnet, the poet is grateful for the subject's good wishes, and remarks that it makes the opinions of others meaningless. **Line 1,** *impression fill*: ie, removed the brand described in Sonnet 111 and alluded to in the following line. **Line 2,** *vulgar scandal*: public disgrace. **Line 3,** *well or ill*: good or bad. (The common pronunciation of "well" likely comprised a pun on the name "Will"). **Line 4,** *o'er green*: cover over; *allow*: grant or acknowledge. **Line 5,** *my all the world*: everything I hold dear. **Lines 5-8,** *I must strive...changes right or wrong*: your opinions of me are the only ones that matter to me. (Truth to tell, this passage baffles everybody...editors included). **Line 10,** *Or*: for; *adder's sense*: the image appears to recall the verse in the King James' version Psalm 58, likening the influence of the wicked to "the poison of a serpent; they are like the deaf adder that stoppeth her ear." **Line 12,** *neglect*: indifference, or lack of attention. **Lines 13-14,** *You are so strongly...methinks are dead*: you are such a part of my being that nobody else matters to me.

113

Since I left you, mine eye is in my mind,
And that which governs me to go about
Doth part his function and is partly blind,
Seems seeing, but effectually is out.
For it no form delivers to the heart
Of bird of flower, or shape, which it doth latch;
Of his quick objects hath the mind no part,
Nor his own vision holds what it doth catch.
For, if it see the rudest or gentlest sight,
The most sweet favor or deformed'st creature,
The mountain or the sea, the day or night,
The crow or dove, it shapes them to your feature.
  Incapable of more, replete with you,
  My most true mind thus makes mine eye untrue.

NOTES: Though they may be separated, the poet finds that everything reminds him of the subject. **Line 1,** *my mine eye is in my mind*: the line plays upon the image of the "mind's eye," noting that the separation has taken his perception inward, into his mind. **Line 2,** *that which governs me to go about*: ie, my eyesight, which guides me. **Line 3,** *Doth part his function*: divides its function. **Line 4,** *effectually*: really, or actually; *out*: extinguished, or departed. **Line 5,** *form*: image. **Line 6,** *latch*: perceive. **Line 7,** *quick*: living, or vivid; *part*: portion or share. **Line 8,** *vision*:perception; *holds*: retains; *catch*: perceive. **Line 10,** *most sweet favor*: prettiest face. **Line 12,** *feature*: form or shape. **Line 14,** *true:* constant or faithful; *untrue*: unreliable. The original text reads "thus maketh mine untrue;" the change is given to render the meaning clear, as well as to maintain the meter of the verse.

114

Or whether doth my mind, being crowned with you,
Drink up the monarch's plague, this flattery?
Or whether shall I say, mine eye saith true,
And that your love taught it this alchemy,
To make of monsters and things indigest
Such cherubins as your sweet self resemble,
Creating every bad a perfect best,
As fast as objects to his beams assemble?
O,'tis the first; 'tis flattery in my seeing,
And my great mind most kingly drinks it up.
Mine eye well knows what with his gust is 'greeing,
And to his palate doth prepare the cup.
   If it be poisoned, 'tis the lesser sin
   That mine eye loves it, and doth first begin.

NOTES: Continuing the previous sonnet, the poet concludes that his continuing perceptions of the subject are only pleasant delusions. **Line 1,** *Or whether doth my mind*: is it that my mind. **Line 2,** *the monarch's plague, this flattery*: ie, distorting the truth or spinning the facts to make them seem more agreeable. (Powerful people did not like unpleasant news any more in Elizabethan England than they do today). **Line 4,** *alchemy*: the transformation of base metals into gold. **Line 5,** *things ingest*: shapeless or formless things. **Line 6,** *cherubins*: cherubins were among the orders of angels in heaven. **Line 8,** *beams*: eyesight. **Line 9,** *'tis flatter in my seeing*: my eyes are deceiving me. **Line 10,** *most kingly drinks it up*: ie, like a monarch falling for flattery. **Line 11,** *gust*: taste. **Lines 13-14:** the image suggested is that of the king's servant, tasting the poisoned wine of deception; the thought conveyed is that the eye's culpability (for letting the king—ie, the mind—drink the poison) is lessened by being deceived.

115

Those lines that I before have writ do lie,
Even those that said I could not love you dearer.
Yet then my judgment knew no reason why
My most full flame should afterwards burn clearer.
But reckoning time, whose millioned accidents
Creep in 'twixt vows and change decrees of kings,
Tan sacred beauty, blunt the sharp'st intents,
Divert strong minds to th' course of altering things:
Alas, why, fearing of time's tyranny
Might I not then say now I love you best,
When I was certain o'er incertainty,
Crowning the present, doubting of the rest?
  Love is a babe; then might I not say so,
  To give full growth to that which still doth grow?

NOTES: The poet laments that his constantly growing love for the subject has turned many of his past verses—those proclaiming his the ultimate love and devotion—into lies. **Line 1,** *Those lines...do lie*: my previous verses on the subject are wrong. **Line 2,** *Even*: precisely or specifically. **Line 4,** *most full flame*: intense passion; *clearer*: more intensely. **Line 5,** *reckoning Time*: keeping Time's power in mind; *accidents*: unforeseen events. **Line 6,** *Creep in 'twixt vows*: interfere with keeping promise. **Line 7,** *Tan sacred beauty*: white was the color of purity as well as beauty (well, at least well-to-do beauty; pretty working-class girls were probably just as tanned as their brothers, even in Elizabethan times); *blut the sharp'st intents*: dull the most intense sense of purpose. **Line 8,** *Divert strong minds...altering things*: make strong-willed people change with changing circumstances. **Line 10,** *then*: at that time. **Line 11,** *certain o'er uncertainty*: beyond doubt. **Line 12,** *Crowning*: deeming supreme, or glorifying. **Lines 13-14:** comparing love to a child, the poet notes that his mistake comes from forgetting that, like a baby, love keeps growing.

116

Let me not to the marriage of true minds
Admit impediments. Love is not love
Which alters when it alteration finds,
Or bends with the remover to remove.
O no! it is an ever-fixèd mark
That looks on tempests and is never shaken;
It is the star to every wandering bark,
Whose worth's unknown, although his height be taken.
Love's not Time's fool, though rosy lips and cheeks
Within his bending sickle's compass come.
Love alters not with his brief hours and weeks,
But bears it out even to the edge of doom.
   If this be error and upon me proved,
   I never writ, nor no man ever loved.

NOTES: Perhaps Shakespeare's greatest sonnet, the poet here remarks in clear and simple language on the eternal and unchanging nature of true love between kindred spirits. **Line 5,** *ever-fixèd*: eternal; *mark:* a seamark—ie, a lighthouse of beacon. **Line 7,** *the star*: Polaris, the pole star; *wandering bark*: lost ship. **Line 12,** *doom*: ie, Doomsday.

117

Accuse me thus: that I have scanted all
Wherein I should your great deserts repay,
Forgot upon your dearest love to call,
Whereto all bonds do tie me day by day;
That I have frequent been with unknown minds,
And given to time your own dear-purchased right;
That I have hoisted sail to all the winds
Which should transport me farthest from your sight.
Book both my wilfulness and errors down,
And on just proof surmise accumulate.
Bring me within the level of your frown,
But shoot not at me in your wakened hate,
   Since my appeal says I did strive to prove
   The constancy and virtue of your love.

NOTES: Noting his own inadequacies, the poet acknowledges that his failings test the constancy of the subject's love. **Line 1,** *scanted*: neglected. **Line 2,** *great deserts*: inestimable worthiness. **Line 4,** *Whereto*: to which. **Line 5,** *unknown minds*: strangers. **Line 6,** *given to time*: wasted. **Line 7,** *hosted sail*: departed from or abandoned. **Line 9,** *Book*: record or write; *wilfulness*: self-indulgence. **Line 10,** *And on just proof surmise accumulate*: and add suspicion to proven facts. **Line 11,** *Bring me within the level of your frown*: aim your frown at me. **Line 13,** *appeal*: defense.

118

Like as to make our appetites more keen,
With eager compounds we our palate urge,
As to prevent our maladies unseen
We sicken to shun sickness when we purge.
Even so, being full of your ne'er-cloying sweetness,
To bitter sauces did I frame my feeding
And, sick of welfare, found a kind of meetness
To be diseased ere that there was true needing.
Thus policy in love, to anticipate
The ills that were not, grew to faults assured,
And brought to medicine a healthful state
Which, rank of goodness, would by ill be cured.
  But thence I learn, and find the lesson true,
  Drugs poison him that so fell sick of you.

NOTES: The poet seeks to excuse his infidelities by claiming that as taking medicines to purge oneself on occasion is an aid to good health, indulging in some occasional "bitter sauces" may be necessary to maintain his fitness in love. **Line 2,** *eager compounds:* ie, purging compounds. **Line 4,** *We sicken to shun sickness when we purge:* ie, we deliberately make ourselves sick to keep ourselves healthy. (The modern practice of some supermodels in purging to maintain their figures would probably strike Elizabethans as equally odd). **Line 6,** *feeding:* diet (carnal as well as culinary). **Line 7,** *meetness:* fittingness or propriety. **Line 9,** *policy:* prudence or craftiness. **Line 10,** *faults assured:* real disorders. **Line 11,** *brought to medicine:* ie, made sick. **Line 12,** *rank:* sated or overfull.

119

What potions have I drunk of Siren tears,
Distilled from limbecks foul as hell within,
Applying fears to hopes and hopes to fears,
Still losing when I saw myself to win!
What wretched errors hath my heart committed,
Whilst it hath thought itself so blessèd never!
How have mine eyes out of their spheres been fitted
In the distraction of this madding fever!
O benefit of ill! now I find true
That better is by evil still made better.
And ruined love, when it is built anew,
Grows fairer than at first, more strong, far greater.
   So I return, rebuked to my content,
   And gain by ill thrice more than I have spent.

NOTES: Searching for poetic silver linings, the poet insists that the various amorous illnesses and medicines to which he subjected himself in the previous sonnet has remade his love into something stronger than ever. **Line 1,** *Siren*: in Greek mythology, the Sirens were supernatural creatures who lured mariners to their destruction with their beautifully seductive singing. **Line 2,** *limbecks*: stills. **Line 3,** *Applying*: administering, ie medicinally. **Line 4,** *Still*: always. **Line 5,** *errors*: sins. **Line 6,** *so blessed never*: blessed to the utmost degree. **Line 7,** *fitted*: sent into fits or convulsions. **Line 8,** *madding*: raging, or delirium-producing. **Line 10,** *better is by evil still made better*: evil can make good stronger.

120

That you were once unkind befriends me now,
And for that sorrow, which I then did feel,
Needs must I under my transgression bow,
Unless my nerves were brass or hammered steel.
For if you were by my unkindness shaken
As I by yours, you've passed a hell of time,
And I, a tyrant, have no leisure taken
To weigh how once I suffered in your crime.
O, that our night of woe might have remembered
My deepest sense, how hard true sorrow hits,
And soon to you, as you to me, then tendered
The humble salve which wounded bosoms fits!
   But that your trespass now becomes a fee;
   Mine ransoms yours, and yours must ransom me.

NOTES: The poet recalls past unkindnesses which the subject has shown, but reassures himself that true friendship heals and overcomes such slights. **Line 1,** *befriends*: benefits or reassures. **Line 2,** *for*: because of, or in exchange for. **Line 3,** *Needs must*: necessarily. **Line 4,** *nerves*: sinews. **Line 6,** *passed a hell of time*: endured endless suffering. **Line 7,** *leisure*: chance or opportunity. **Line 8,** *weigh*: consider; *in your crime*: by your offense. **Line 9,** *remembered*: reminded. **Line 12,** *humble salve*: the healing balm of humility. **Line 13,** *fee*: payment. **Line 14,** *ransoms, ransom*: pays or atones for.

121

'Tis better to be vile than vile esteemed,
When not to be receives reproach of being
And the just pleasure lost, which is so deemed
Not by our feeling, but by others' seeing.
For why should others' false adulterate eyes
Give salutation to my sportive blood?
Or on my frailties why are frailer spies,
Which in their wills count bad what I think good?
No, I am that I am, and they that level
At my abuses reckon up their own.
I may be straight, though they themselves be bevel,
By their rank thoughts my deeds must not be shown,
  Unless this general evil they maintain:
  All men are bad, and in their badness reign.

NOTES: Noting that, all things considered, it is better to be wicked than simply thought so, the poet acknowledges his failings, but remarks that he is no worse than his detractors. **Line 1,** *vile*: wicked; *vile esteemed*: thought to be wicked. **Line 3,** *just pleasure*: the pleasure that comes from legitimate wickedness. **Line 4,** *by others' seeing*: being deemed so by others. **Line 6,** *my sportive blood*: my lively (ie, amorous) nature. *Line 7, frailties*: weaknesses. **Line 8,** *Which*: who. **Line 9,** *I am that I am*: I stand by my actions; *level*: aim. **Line 10,** *my abuses*: my moral failings. **Line 11,** *straight*: honest; *bevel*: slanted, or dishonest. **Line 12,** *rank*: lustful; *must not be shown*: should not be taken as proven. **Line 13,** *maintain*: assert or claim.

122

Thy gift, thy tables, are within my brain
Full charactered with lasting memory,
Which shall above that idle rank remain
Beyond all date, even to eternity.
Or, at the least, so long as brain and heart
Have faculty by nature to subsist,
Till each to razed oblivion yield his part
Of thee, thy record never can be missed.
That poor retention could not so much hold,
Nor need I tallies thy dear love to score.
Therefore to give them from me was I bold,
To trust those tables that receive thee more.
   To keep an adjunct to remember thee
   Were to import forgetfulness in me.

NOTES: The poet tries to explain away his actions in giving away a gift of a writing tablet he received from the subject, possibly containing sentiments expressed by the subject. (Unfortunately, the best he could do was to insist that keeping them would have implied that he needed help remembering). **Line 1,** *tables*: notebooks; *within my brain*: imprinted on my mind. **Line 2,** *charactered*: inscribed. **Line 3,** *above*: superior to; *idle rank*:: inert or meaningless pages. **Line 6,** *faculty*: capacity. **Line 7,** *razed oblivion*: nothingness. **Line 8,** *thy record*: the memory of you. **Line 9,** *retention*: the receptacle for your memory— ie, the notebook. **Line 10,** *tallies*: a record of sums of money owed; *score*: record. (The image is one of a tally-stick, on which notches were carved to represent debts owed). **Line 11,** *to give them from me*: to give them away; *was I bold*: I dared. **Line 12,** *To trust...thee more*: trusting instead to the superior tablet of my own memory. **Line 13,** *adjunct*: memento. **Line 14,** *import*: imply.

123

No! Time, thou shalt not boast that I do change.
Thy pyramids built up with newer might
To me are nothing novel, nothing strange;
They are but dressings of a former sight.
Our dates are brief, and therefore we admire
What thou dost foist upon us that is old,
And rather make them born to our desire
Than think that we before have heard them told.
Thy registers and thee I both defy,
Not wondering at the present nor the past,
For thy recórds, and what we see, doth lie,
Made more or less by thy continual haste.
  This I do vow, and this shall ever be:
  I will be true, despite thy scythe and thee.

NOTES: Returning to the theme that there is really nothing new under the sun, the poet observes that it is only the shortness of our lives that make us view things as new or novel. **Line 2,** *pyramids*: the image suggested is anything grand or spectacular built by Man. **Line 4,** *dressings of a former sight*: new versions of things we have seen before. **Line 5,** *Our dates are brief*: our lives are short. **Lines 6-8,** *What thou...have heard them told*: those tired, old things that you fool us into thinking is new, taking advantage of our desire to see them as new. **Line 9,** *registers*: records. **Line 11,** *thy recórds...doth lie*: the annuls of history and our own perceptions are both deceiving. **Line 12,** *Made more or less*: exaggerated and lessened. **Line 14,** *scythe*: the image is of Father Time or the grim reaper.

124

If my dear love were but the child of state,
It might for fortune's bastard be unfathered,
As subject to time's love or to time's hate,
Weeds among weeds, or flowers with flowers gathered.
No, it was builded far from accident;
It suffers not in smiling pomp, nor falls
Under the blow of thrallèd discontent
Whereto the inviting time our fashion calls.
It fears not policy, that heretic,
Which works on leases of short-numbered hours,
But all alone stands hugely politic,
That it nor grows with heat nor drowns with showers.
    To this I witness call the fools of time,
        Which die for goodness, who have lived for crime.

NOTES: The poet remarks on the constancy of his love, in the face of ever-changing circumstances. **Line 1,** *child of state*: an accidental child, ie, born of circumstances. **Line 2,** *unfathered*: neglected as a bastard. **Line 3,** *As subject...time's hate*: subject to favor or disfavor with changing circumstances. **Line 5,** *builded*: built; *accident*: chance or circumstance. **Line 6,** *suffers not in*: is unaffected by. **Line 7,** *thrallèd*: subjugated. **Line 8,** *inviting*: beckoning; *fashion*: current public fancy. **Line 9,** *policy*: expedience, or scheming; *heretic*: one who shifts allegiance away from truth for the sake of expediency. **Line 11,** *But all alone...hugely politic*: it (ie, love) stands apart, wise and independent. **Line 14,** *Which die for goodness, who have lived for crime*: those who, being executed as criminals, proclaim themselves dying for a holy cause.

125

Were't aught to me I bore the canopy,
With my extern the outward honoring,
Or laid great bases for eternity,
Which proves more short than waste or ruining?
Have I not seen dwellers on form and favor
Lose all, and more, by paying too much rent
For compound sweet, forgoing simple savor,
Pitiful thrivers, in their gazing spent?
No, let me be obsequious in thy heart,
And take thou my oblation, poor but free,
Which is not mixed with seconds, knows no art,
But mutual render, only me for thee.
  Hence, thou suborned informer: a true soul
  When most impeached stands least in thy control.

NOTES: The poet insists that his private devotion is more honorable than showy displays of public affection. **Line 1,** *Were't aught:* would it matter; *bore the canopy:* showed outward signs of respect. (On formal occasions, the monarch would be carried in a canopy borne by courtiers). **Line 2,** *extern:* outward appearance. **Line 3,** *laid great bases for eternity:* erected massive foundations intended to last for all time. **Line 4,** *waste or ruining:* the forces of destruction or decay. **Line 5,** *dwellers on form and favor:* flatterers who pay careful attention to ceremony in hopes of gaining favor with the powerful. **Line 8,** *thrivers, in their gazing spent:* ambitious people who lose everything while trying to gain favor. **Line 9,** *obsequious:* attentive, or fawning. **Line 10,** *oblation:* offering. **Line 11,** *not mixed with seconds:* free of ulterior motives. **Line 12,** *render:* tender or exchange. **Line 13,** *suborned:* corrupt, ie, perjured or lying. **Line 14,** *impeached:* accused; *control:* power.

126

O thou, my lovely boy, who in thy power
Dost hold Time's fickle glass, his sickle hour;
Who hast by waning grown, and therein show'st
Thy lovers withering as thy sweet self grow'st;
If Nature, sovereign mistress over wrack,
As thou goest onwards still will pluck thee back.
She keeps thee to this purpose, that her skill
May time disgrace, and wretched minutes kill.
Yet fear her, O thou minion of her pleasure!
She may detain, but not still keep, her treasure.
Her audit, though delayed, answered must be,
And her quietus is to render thee.

NOTES: This verse, like Sonnet 99, departs from conventional form: it has twelve
lines, consisting of rhymed couplets. It also appears to be the last Sonnet written
to the "fair youth" of earlier verses, warning him that while he may be Nature's
favorite, Time—ie, death and old age—will eventually claim all things. **Line 2,**
time's fickle glass: time's hourglass; sickle hour: the time at which growing things
are harvested. **Line 3,** *hast by waning grown*: has become more beautiful with age
and maturity. **Line 4,** *lovers*: friends, or paramours. **Line 5,** *wrack*: ruin. **Line 6,**
pluck: snatch, or pull. **Line 7,** *disgrace*: mock, or put to shame. **Line 8,** *minutes*: the
original text reads "minute." **Line 9,** *minion*; favorite. **Line 10,** *still*: forever. **Line
11,** *Her audit*: Nature's accounting to Time. **Line 12,** *her quietus is to render thee*: she
(ie, Nature) will close her account by surrendering you in payment.

127

In the old age black was not counted fair,
Or if it were, it bore not beauty's name.
But now is black beauty's successive heir,
And beauty slandered with a bastard shame,
For since each hand hath put on nature's power,
Fairing the foul with art's false borrowed face,
Sweet beauty hath no name, no holy bower,
But is profaned, if not lives in disgrace.
Therefore, my mistress' eyes are raven black,
Her eyes so suited, and they mourners seem
At such who, not born fair, no beauty lack,
Slandering creation with a false esteem.
   Yet so they mourn, becoming of their woe,
   That every tongue says beauty should look so.

NOTES: In the opening sonnet of the sequence directed toward the "dark lady,"
the poet notes that she does not meet the conventional standard of beauty—fair
(or blond) hair and light skin—even though that standard can be met by the use
of cosmetics, ie, "art's false borrowed face." (Men, it seems, were just as easily
distracted by feminine enhancements in Elizabethan times as ever). **Line 1,** *old age*:
times past; *black*: dark (of hair or skin or heart); *fair*: beautiful. (The line employs
wordplays on all meanings of both terms). **Line 2,** *bore not beauty's name*: was not
admitted to be beautiful. (The implication, here and in the lines that follow, is of
illegitimacy or unacknowledged birth). **Line 3,** *successive*: ie, next in order of
succession, ie, legitimate. **Line 4,** *bastard shame*: the shame of being thought
illegitimate. **Line 6,** *Fairing the foul*: making the ugly beautiful; *art's false borrowed face*:
the use of cosemetics. **Line 10,** *suited*: matched. **Line 7,** *hath no name*: is illegitimate,
or unrecognized. **Line 11,** *such who, not born fair, not beauty lack*: those who, although
not born pretty, have managed to make themselves beautiful.

128

How oft, when thou, my music, music play'st
Upon that blessèd wood, whose motion sounds
With thy sweet fingers, when thou gently sway'st
The wiry concord that mine ear confounds,
Do I envy those jacks that nimble leap
To kiss the tender inward of thy hand,
Whilst my poor lips, which should that harvest reap,
At the wood's boldness by thee blushing stand.
To be so tickled, they would change their state
And situation with those dancing chips,
O'er whom thy fingers walk with gentle gait,
Making dead wood more blest than living lips.
　Since saucy jacks so happy are in this,
　Give them thy fingers, me thy lips to kiss.

NOTES: The poet wishes himself transformed into a keyboard played by the subject. **Line 2,** *wood*: the reference is to a virginal, a keyboard instrument of the Elizabethan era resembling a harpsichord. **Line 4,** *concord*: harmony. (The concord is "wiry" because of the wires of the instrument, not because the harmonies are thin); *confounds*: overwhelms. **Line 5,** *jacks*: keys. **Line 13,** *saucy*: impudent. ("Jacks" is also another word for "fellows," leading to a clever pun).

129

The expense of spirit in a waste of shame
Is lust in action, and till action, lust
Is perjured, murderous, bloody, full of blame,
Savage, extreme, rude, cruel, not to trust,
Enjoyed no sooner but despisèd straight,
Past reason hunted, and no sooner had,
Past reason hated as a swallowed bait
On purpose laid to make the taker mad.
Mad in pursuit and in possession so;
Had, having, and in quest to have, extreme—
A bliss in proof, and proved, a very woe;
Before, a joy proposed; behind, a dream.
    All this the world well knows; yet none knows well
    To shun the heaven that leads men to this hell.

NOTES: One of Shakespeare's most obviously bawdy poems, here the poet
expresses the dark side of sexuality, noting that the madness of lust often results
in self-loathing, and resentment toward the "quarry" for being such an irresistible
lure. **Line 1,** *expense*: consumption or use; *spirit*: power or energy (also the
expression of bodily fluids, including seminal fluids, thought to emanate from the
heart); *waste of shame*: a shameful waste, or a needlessly shameful act. **Line 3,** *blame*:
guilt. **Line 4,** *rude*: violent; *not to trust*: not to be trusted. **Line 5,** *straight*: immedi-
ately. (Also, a possibly obscene pun continued in the ensuing lines). **Lines 6-7,**
reason: Booth suggests a likely pun stemming from the Elizabethan pronunciation
of "reason"—which would sound like "raisin" the dried fruit, as well as "rai-
sin'"...with obvious connotations in poem about lust. See Booth, Shakespeare's
Sonnets, 445. **Line 11,** *A bliss...a very woe*: delightful in the execution, but having
been done a source of grief. **Line 12,** *Before*: in anticipation; *behind*: in hindsight.
Line 14, *heaven*: bliss; *hell*: agony or grief.

130

My mistress' eyes are nothing like the sun;
Coral is far more red than her lips' red;
If snow be white, why then her breasts are dun;
If hairs be wires, black wires grow on her head.
I have seen roses damasked, red and white,
But no such roses see I in her cheeks;
And in some perfumes is there more delight
Than in the breath that from my mistress reeks.
I love to hear her speak, yet well I know
That music hath a far more pleasing sound.
I grant I never saw a goddess go;
My mistress, when she walks, treads on the ground.
   And yet, by heaven, I think my love as rare
   As any she belied with false compare.

NOTES: The poet pokes fun at several poetic cliches, concluding that the subject is as lovely as any woman—even if she defies all the usual similes. **Line 3,** *dun*: dull or gray. **Line 4,** *wires*: poets of earlier days often compared golden hair to golden wires, or beaten gold used in jewelry or embroidery. (Telegraphs and barbed wire, which might come immediately to the mind of the modern reader, were still some years in the future when Shakespeare was writing). **Line 5,** *damasked*: patterned. **Line 8,** *reeks*: emanates. (Actually, the connotation is not nearly as distasteful as it might seem to the modern reader: Elizabethans were more concerned with the vapor emitted, rather than the quality or strength of the emanation, and the verb was largely neutral on the content). **Line 11,** *go*: walk. **Line 13,** *by heaven*: I swear under heaven. **Line 13,** *rare*: splendid, as well as uncommon **Line 14,** *As any...false compare*: as any woman flattered by insincere praise.

131

Thou art as tyrannous, so as thou art,
As those whose beauties proudly make them cruel.
For well thou know'st to my dear doting heart
Thou art the fairest and most precious jewel.
Yet, in good faith, some say that thee behold
Thy face hath not the power to make love groan.
To say they err I dare not be so bold,
Although I swear it to myself alone.
And, to be sure that is not false, I swear
A thousand groans but thinking on thy face.
One on another's neck do witness bear,
Thy black is fairest in my judgment's place.
  In nothing art thou black, save in thy deeds;
  And thence this slander, as I think, proceeds.

NOTES: Here, the poet skewers his mistress while defending her loveliness against attack: she is really quite pretty, he concludes; it is only her behavior that is unattractive. **Line 1,** *so as thou art*: being as you are. **Lines 5-6,** *some say that thee behold...make love groan*: some who see you insist that you are not pretty enough to make men swoon. **Line 7,** *say*: ie, say in public. **Line 8,** *to myself alone*: in private. **Line 9,** *to be sure that*: as evidence that; *false*: ie, a falsehood. **Line 11,** *One on another's neck*: one after the other. **Line 12,** *Thy black*: your darkness. **Line 13,** *black*: wicked or immoral; *save in thy deeds*: except in your behavior. **Line 14,** *this slander*: ie, the claim that the subject's face "hath not the power to make love groan."

132

Thine eyes I love, and they, as pitying me,
Knowing thy heart torments me with disdain,
Have put on black, and loving mourners be,
Looking with pretty ruth upon my pain.
And truly not the morning sun of heaven
Better becomes the grey cheeks of the east,
Nor that full star that ushers in the even
Doth half that glory to the sober west
As those two mourning eyes become thy face.
O, let it then as well beseem thy heart
To mourn for me, since mourning doth thee grace,
And suit thy pity like in every part.
   Then will I swear beauty herself is black,
   And all they foul that thy complexion lack.

NOTES: Again defying conventional notions of loveliness, the poet insists that as the subject's dark eyes shows her pity for the pain of his own devotion, her darkened heart would show her compassion for his own. **Line 1,** *as*: as if. **Line 4,** *ruth*: compassion or pity. **Line 6,** *Better becomes*: is more becoming to; *the grey cheeks of the east*: the dawning day. **Line 7,** *that full star*: ie, Venus; *even*: evening. **Line 8,** *sober*: somber or subdued. **Line 10,** *beseem*: befit. **Line 11,** *mourning doth thee grace*: black (the color of mourning) suits or compliments you. **Line 12,** *suit thy pity like in every part*: dress your pity in black, like the rest of you. **Line 14,** *foul*: ugly.

133

Beshrew that heart that makes my heart to groan
For that deep wound it gives my friend and me!
Is't not enough to torture me alone,
But slave to slavery my sweet'st friend must be?
Me from myself thy cruel eye hath taken,
And my next self thou harder hast engrossed.
Of him, myself, and thee, I am forsaken,
A torment thrice threefold thus to be crossed.
Prison my heart in thy steel bosom's ward,
But then my friend's heart let my poor heart bail.
Whoe'er keeps me, let my heart be his guard;
Thou canst not then use rigor in my jail.
  And yet thou wilt; for I, being pent in thee,
  Perforce am thine, and all that is in me.

NOTES: It is widely thought that this sonnet and the next one were written at the same time as Sonnets 40-42, in which the poet is addressing a friend seduced by the poet's own mistress—a fact which, he tells the mistress, makes his own torment even crueler. **Line 1,** *Beshrew*: may evil befall. **Line 2,** *deep wound*: serious injury. **Line 4,** *slavery*: ie, abject devotion. (It seems that Elizabethan lovers were often languishing in carnal servitude of one sort or another). **Line 6,** *next self*: closest friend; *engrossed*: taken possession of. **Line 8,** *crossed*: thwarted. **Line 9,** *Prison*: imprison; *ward*: cell. **Line 10,** *bail*: cause to be set free, or redeem; also, confine or constrict. **Line 12,** *rigor*: harshness. **Line 13,** *pent*: confined. **Line 14,** *Perforce*: necessarily.

134

So, now I have confessed that he is thine,
And I myself am mortgaged to thy will,
Myself I'll forfeit, so that other mine
Thou wilt restore, to be my comfort still.
But thou wilt not, nor he will not be free,
For thou art covetous, and he is kind.
He learned but surety-like to write for me
Under that bond that him as fast doth bind.
The statute of thy beauty thou wilt take,
Thou usurer, that put'st forth all to use,
And sue a friend came debtor for my sake,
So him I lose through my unkind abuse.
 Him have I lost; thou hast both him and me.
 He pays the whole, and yet am I not free.

NOTES: This sonnet continues the carnal dilemma described in the previous verse, employing the imagery of ledgers, finance, and accounting. **Line 2,** *mortgaged*: pledged; *will*: intentions, or carnal desire. **Line 3,** *forfeit*: surrender as a penalty; *that other mine*: my other self. **Line 5,** *nor he will not be*: nor does he wish to be. **Line 7,** *surety-like to write for me*: to sign for me as a surety. **Line 10,** *usurer*: one who lends money; *put'st forth all to use*: lay out all to use for profit; "use" was also a common euphemism meaning "to use sexually." **Line 11,** *sue*: to bring suit against; or to woo; *came*: who became. **Line 12,** *my unkind abuse*: the ill usage I have received (at your hands), or my ill usage (of my friend). **Line 14,** *the whole*: the entire debt. (And the bawdy pun is undoubtedly intended).

135

Whoever hath her wish, thou hast thy will,
And will to boot, and will in overplus;
More than enough am I that vex thee still,
To thy sweet will making addition thus.
Wilt thou, whose will is large and spacious,
Not once vouchsafe to hide my will in thine?
Shall will in others seem right gracious,
And in my will no fair acceptance shine?
The sea, all water, yet receives rain still,
And in abundance addeth to his store;
So thou, being rich in will, add to thy will
One will of mine, to make thy large will more.
   Let no unkind, no fair beseechers kill;
   Think all but one, and me in that one will.

NOTES: The romping friskiness of the "wills" in this and the following sonnet play with multiple notions of the word—from the poet's name, to sexual desire, to the fact that its pronunciation in Shakespeare's day sounded like the word "well," which was a bawdy euphemism for the female sex organ. (It also presents something of a problem for those who insist that someone else wrote everything ascribed to Shakespeare, since there would otherwise be no real point to all the puns). An exploration of some of the bawdier aspects of these sonnets is found in Booth, *Shakespeare's Sonnets*, pp 466–473. It is probably enough for the reader to understand that the poet intends each sense of the word that a salacious imagination can devise...and probably a few more along the way. **Line 1,** *thou hast thy will*: in addition to the obvious pun on the poet's name, the line recounts the various proverbs about women and their wills. **Line 2,** *to boot*: also (as in modern usage; it does not seem to be an invitation to kick the poet). **Line 9,** *The sea...rain still*: the line suggests various proverbs about the sea refusing no river.

136

If thy soul check thee that I come so near,
Swear to thy blind soul that I was thy will,
And will, thy soul knows, is admitted there.
Thus far for love, my love-suit, sweet fulfill,
Will will fulfill the treasure of thy love—
Aye, fill it full with wills, and my will one.
In things of great receipt with ease we prove,
Among a number one is reckoned none.
Then in the number let me pass untold,
Though in thy store's account I one must be.
For nothing hold me, so it please thee hold
That nothing me, a something, sweet, to thee.
  Make but my name thy love, and love that still,
  And then thou lovest me, for my name is Will.

NOTES: This verse continues the thoroughly bawdy "Will-full" pun motif. (The various fillings that accompany the poet's "love-suit," or "fulfill" the subject's "treasure" do not arise innocently). **Line 1,** *check*: chastise or rebuke. **Line 3,** *admitted*: allowed to enter. **Line 4,** *for love*: out of charity. **Line 5,** *treasure*: ie, treasure chest. **Line 7,** *things*: items (in Shakespeare's day, "thing" was, like "well," also a slang term for the genitals); *receipt*: capacity or extent. **Line 8,** *number*: ie, a large number. **Line 9,** *in the number*: among the multitudes. **Line 10,** *thy store's account*: your (carnal) inventory. **Line 11,** *For nothing hold me*: consider me as nothing. **Line 12,** *nothing, something*: "thing" was a slang term for male genitals, as well as the female variety. **Line 13,** *my name*: ie, "Will" (either in person, or by desire).

137

Thou blind fool, Love, what dost thou to mine eyes
That they behold, and see not what they see?
They know what beauty is, see where it lies,
Yet what the best is, take the worst to be.
If eyes, corrupt by over-partial looks,
Be anchored in the bay where all men ride,
Why of eyes' falsehood hast thou forgèd hooks,
Whereto the judgment of my heart is tied?
Why should my heart think that a several plot,
Which my heart knows the wide world's common place?
Or mine eyes, seeing this, say this is not,
To put fair truth upon so foul a face?
   In things right true my heart and eyes have erred,
   And to this false plague are they now transferred.

NOTES: Complaining about the object of his affections, the poet blames Cupid for leading him astray. **Line 1,** *Love*: Cupid. **Line 3,** *lies*: is found, or deceives. **Line 4,** *what the best is take the worst to be*: ie, take the worst for the best. **Line 5,** *corrupt*: corrupted; *over-partial*: biased. **Line 6,** *ride*: lie anchored, or copulate. (The type of "anchor" and location of the "bay" will vary, accordingly). **Line 7,** *eyes' falsehood*: misleading amorous glances; *forgèd*: made, or counterfeited. **Line 9,** *several*: private. **Line 10,** *common*: public. **Line 11,** *seeing*: recognizing. **Line 12,** *put*: attribute; truth: honor, or beauty. **Line 14,** *false plague*: affliction of false perceptions.

138

When my love swears that she is made of truth
I do believe her, though I know she lies,
That she might think me some untutored youth,
Unlearnèd in the world's false subtleties.
Thus, vainly thinking that she thinks me young,
Although she knows my days are past the best,
Simply I credit her false speaking tongue;
On both sides thus is simple truth suppressed.
But wherefore says she not she is unjust?
And wherefore say not I that I am old?
O, love's best habit is in seeming trust,
And age in love loves not to have years told.
   Therefore I lie with her and she with me,
   And in our faults by lies we flattered be.

NOTES: Here, the poet suggests the wisdom of honest and open deception as a source of mutual happiness between lovers. **Line 1,** *made of truth*: is faithful and true. **Line 2,** *lies*: is lying; or, lies with other men. **Line 3,** *untutored*: innocent or naive. **Line 5,** *vainly*: foolishly; or conceitedly; or in vain. **Line 7,** *Simply*: credulously; *credit*: believe. **Line 8,** *suppressed*: hidden, or unrevealed. **Line 9,** *unjust*: unfaithful, or untruthful. **Line 11,** *habit*: a garment, as well as a customary mode of behavior; *seeming trust*: outward credulity. **Line 12,** *age in love*: infatuated older people. **Lines 13-14,** *lie; lies*: both senses of "lie" are meant—carnal as well as untruthfulness (Shakespeare's best puns often could not help being bawdy); *faults*: failings or shortcomings.

139

O, call not me to justify the wrong
That thy unkindness lays upon my heart.
Wound me not with thine eye but with thy tongue.
Use power with power and slay me not by art.
Tell me thou lovest elsewhere; but in my sight,
Dear heart, forbear to glance thine eye aside.
What need'st thou wound with cunning when thy might
Is more than my o'er-pressed defense can bide?
Let me excuse thee: ah! my love well knows
Her pretty looks have been mine enemies,
And therefore from my face she turns my foes,
That they elsewhere might dart their injuries.
    Yet do not so; but since I am near slain,
    Kill me outright with looks, and rid my pain.

NOTES: Lamenting the subject's cruelty, the poet begs her to kill him at last with her deadliest weapons—her eyes. **Line 4,** *with power*: ie, forcefully or powerfully; *art*: artifice or cunning. **Line 5,** *elsewhere*: someone else; *in my sight*: in my presence. **Line 6,** *glance thine eye*: turn your gaze. **Line 7,** *might*: power. **Line 8,** *o'er-pressed*: over-burdened; bide: withstand. **Line 9,** *excuse*: justify. **Line 10,** *looks*: glances, or appearance. **Line 11,** *she turns my foes*: she averts her eyes. **Line 13,** *near*: nearly. **Line 14,** *rid*: end.

140

Be wise as thou art cruel; do not press
My tongue-tied patience with too much disdain,
Lest sorrow lend me words and words express
The manner of my pity-wanting pain.
If I might teach thee wit, better it were,
Though not to love, yet, love, to tell me so,
As testy sick men, when their deaths be near,
No news but health from their physicians know.
For if I should despair, I should grow mad,
And in my madness might speak ill of thee.
Now this ill-wresting world is grown so bad,
Mad slanderers by mad ears believèd be.
   That I may not be so, nor thou belied,
   Bear thine eyes straight, though thy proud heart go wide.

NOTES: Continuing the theme of his mistress' cruelty, the poet cautions her against overt contempt, suggesting that a gentle lie about her feelings would prevent him from babbling in despair. **Line 1,** *Be wise as*: be as wise as; *press*: put pressure on. **Line 2,** *tongue-tied*: the imagery invokes the practice of torturing one who refused to enter a plea to a crime by pressing his body with heavy weights until he either pleaded, or died. (See Introduction, pp 116–117). **Line 4,** *pity-wanting*: needing pity. **Line 5,** *wit*: wisdom. **Line 6,** *so*: ie, that you do (love me). **Line 10,** *speak ill of thee*: say bad things about you. **Lines 11-12,** *this ill-wresting world*: this world, eager to believe the worst. **Line 13,** *belied*: slandered. **Line 14,** *straight*: steady; *go wide*: go astray. (The line invokes the image of archery).

141

In faith, I do not love thee with mine eyes,
For they in thee a thousand errors note;
But 'tis my heart that loves what they despise,
Who in despite of view is pleased to dote.
Nor are mine ears with thy tongue's tune delighted,
Nor tender feeling, to base touches prone,
Nor taste, nor smell, desire to be invited
To any sensual feast with thee alone.
But my five wits, nor my five senses, can
Dissuade one foolish heart from serving thee,
Who leaves unswayed the likeness of a man,
Thy proud heart's slave and vassal wretch to be.
  Only my plague thus far I count my gain,
  That she that makes me sin awards me pain.

NOTES: The poet notes that where love is concerned, the heart often overrides
the senses. **Line 1,** *In faith*: truly. **Line 2,** *errors*, defects. **Line 4,** *Who in despite of view*:
which, regardless what my eyes actually see. **Line 5,** *thy tongue's tune*: the sound of
your voice. **Line 6,** *base*: low. **Line 9,** *five wits*: as opposed to the "five senses," the
"five wits" were thought to be common sense, imagination, memory, estimation,
and fantasy. **Line 11,** *unswayed*: undeterred, or lacking self-control. **Line 13,** *my
plague*: my lover's affliction. **Line 14,** *awards me pain*: determines my punishment.

142

Love is my sin and thy dear virtue hate,
Hate of my sin, grounded on sinful loving.
O, but with mine compare thou thine own state,
And thou shalt find it merits not reproving;
Or, if it do, not from those lips of thine,
That have profaned their scarlet ornaments
And sealed false bonds of love as oft as mine,
Robbed others' beds' revénues of their rents.
Be it lawful I love thee, as thou lovest those
Whom thine eyes woo as mine importune thee.
Root pity in thy heart, that when it grows,
Thy pity may deserve to pitied be.
  If thou dost seek to have what thou dost hide,
  By self-example mayst thou be denied.

NOTES: The poet scolds his mistress for her other dalliances, suggesting that it is her other carnal adventures, and not maidenly virtue, that is causing her to spurn his advances. **Line 1,** *virtue*: essence, or predominant characteristic. **Line 2,** *sinful loving*: my own love that is sinful; or your own promiscuity. **Line 6,** *scarlet ornaments*: cosmetic redness. **Line 8,** *other's beds*: the beds of other women; *revénues of their rents*: ie, the sexual relations due to the rightful owners. (The accent is placed on the second syllable to maintain the meter of the line). **Line 11,** *Root*: sow or plant. **Line 12,** *Thy pity*: your own pitiable state. **Line 13,** *what thou dost hide*: ie, pity. **Line 14,** *self-example*: your own example.

143

Lo, as a careful housewife runs to catch
One of her feathered creatures broke away,
Sets down her babe and makes all swift dispatch
In púrsuit of the thing she would have stay,
Whilst her neglected child holds her in chase,
Cries to catch her whose busy care is bent
To follow that which flies before her face,
Not prizing her poor infant's discontent;
So runn'st thou after that which flies from thee,
Whilst I, thy babe, chase thee afar behind.
But if thou catch thy hope, turn back to me
And play the mother's part, kiss me, be kind.
  So will I pray that thou mayst have thy will,
  If thou turn back, and my loud crying still.

NOTES: Here, the poet likens his carnal merry-go-round with his mistress to a baby chasing after its mother...who in turn set the baby down to run after a stray chicken. **Line 1,** *careful*: attentive or distressed; *housewife*: was pronounced "hussif." **Line 2,** *broke away*: which has gotten loose. **Line 5,** *holds her in chase*: chases after her. **Line 8,** *prizing*: noticing. **Line 11,** *thy hope*: what you are seeking. **Line 13,** *thy will*: what you are seeking, or your lust, or the poet (as returneth we to mótif, "Will-fully"). **Line 14,** *still*: calm or pacify.

144

Two loves I have, of comfort and despair,
Which like two spirits do suggest me still.
The better angel is a man right fair,
The worser spirit a woman colored ill.
To win me soon to hell, my female evil
Tempteth my better angel from my side,
And would corrupt my saint to be a devil,
Wooing his purity with her foul pride.
And whether that my angel be turned fiend
Suspect I may, but not directly tell;
But being both from me, both to each friend,
I guess one angel in another's hell.
    Yet this shall I ne'er know, but live in doubt,
    Till my bad angel fire my good one out.

NOTES: In this verse, the poet returns to the theme of sharing a mistress with his friend—whom he casts as a bad angel, and a good one, respectively. **Line 2,** *suggest*: tempt, or prompt; *still*: constantly. **Line 3,** *right fair*: very beautiful (or, light-colored). **Line 4,** *colored ill*: dark. **Line 6,** *side*: the original text reads "sight," which would make the ensuing rhyme (with "pride," in line 8) non-existent—suggesting either a misprint in the original, or a radical restructuring of pronunciation in the ensuing centuries. **Line 8,** *foul pride*: seductive beauty. **Line 9,** *whether that*: if it should come to be. **Line 10,** *directly*: immediately. **Line 11,** *from*: away from; *both to each friend*: mutual friends. **Line 12,** *one angel in another's hell*: each shares the torment of the other; or, one is the other's punishment. **Line 14,** *fire...out*: drives off (either by the tormenting fires of hell...or by the flaming pains of venereal disease).

145

Those lips that Love's own hand did make
Breathed forth the sound that said "I hate"
To me that languished for her sake.
But when she saw my woeful state,
Straight in her heart did mercy come,
Chiding that tongue that ever sweet
Was used in giving gentle doom,
And taught it thus anew to greet.
"I hate" she altered with an end,
That followed it as gentle day
Doth follow night, who like a fiend
From heaven to hell is flown away.
    "I hate" from hate away she threw,
    And saved my life, saying "not you."

NOTES: Alert readers concerned about the missing iamb in each line can relax; this verse actually does contain eight syllables per line. The net effect, however, causes the verse to sound oddly like a greeting card, causing some scholars to hope that this particular sonnet, at least, is not really by Shakespeare. See, Booth, *Shakespeare's Sonnets*, p 500. In any event, it is widely regarded as the weakest in the entire collection, possibly showing a young poet who has not yet blossomed into the immortal writer that we admire today. **Line 1,** *Love's*: Cupid's. **Line 7,** *used*: employed.

146

Poor soul, the center of my sinful earth,
My sinful earth, these rebel powers that thee array,
Why dost thou pine within and suffer dearth,
Painting thy outward walls so costly gay?
Why so large cost, having so short a lease,
Dost thou upon thy fading mansion spend?
Shall worms, inheritors of this excess,
Eat up thy charge? Is this thy body's end?
Then soul, live thou upon thy servant's loss,
And let that pine to aggravate thy store.
Buy terms divine in selling hours of dross;
Within be fed, without be rich no more.
   So shalt thou feed on death, that feeds on men,
   And death once dead, there's no more dying then.

NOTES: Waxing metaphysical, the poet draws upon spiritual notions of body and soul, suggesting that death results in its own downfall, and that the path to eternal life lies not in transient pleasures. **Line 1,** *the center of my sinful earth*: While Copernicus published his revolutionary (and theologically heretical) work detailing the Earth's movements around the sun in 1543, in Shakespeare's day the work was largely unknown, and potentially dangerous to those who agreed with it. Consequently, most Elizabethans still believed that the Earth was the center of the universe, and that all things were drawn toward the center. In this context, the phrase is likening the writer's soul to the center of his own world. **Line 2,** *my sinful earth*: this repetition is widely believed to be a misprint, stemming from one of the earliest folios, which apparently repeated the end of the preceding line rather than the iamb intended to begin the next one. "Pressed with" or "feeding" might give the line its intended meaning—but it is entirely conjecture, as "arming" or "against" would do just as nicely. Unfortunately, no one checked with Shakespeare. **Line 6,** *fading mansion*: ie, body. **Line 7,** *excess*: extravagence. **Line 8,** *charge*: amount spent. **Line 9,** *servant*: ie, the writer's body. **Line 10,** *that*: ie, that body; *pine*: suffer; *aggravate*: increase. **Line 11,** *terms divine*: life immortal.

147

My love is as a fever, longing still
For that which longer nurseth the disease,
Feeding on that which doth preserve the ill,
The uncertain sickly appetite to please.
My reason, the physician to my love,
Angry that his prescriptions are not kept,
Hath left me, and I desperate now approve
Desire is death, which physic did except.
Past cure I am, now reason is past care,
And frantic-mad with evermore unrest;
My thoughts and my discourse as madmen's are,
At random from the truth vainly expressed.
    For I have sworn thee fair, and thought thee bright,
    Who art as black as hell, as dark as night.

NOTES: Here, the poet likens his love for his mistress to an illness. (He was probably not the first man to think along these lines, and certainly not the last). **Lines 1,5,** *love*: infatuation; *longing still*: always longing. **Line 2,** *which longer nurseth*: which prolongs. **Line 3,** *ill*: sickness. **Line 6,** *prescriptions*: instructions. **Line 7,** *desperate*: in despair; *approve*: demonstrate or show. **Line 8,** *physic*: medicine; *except*: forbid or proscribe. **Line 10,** *evermore*: continuous. **Line 11,** *discourse*: speech. **Line 12,** *At random*: haphazardly; *vainly*: foolishly, or futilely.

148

O me, what eyes hath love put in my head,
Which have no correspondence with true sight!
Or, if they have, where is my judgment fled,
That censures falsely what they see aright?
If that be fair whereon my false eyes dote,
What means the world to say it is not so?
If it be not, then love doth well denote
Love's eye is not so true as all men's "No."
How can it? O, how can love's eye be true,
That is so vexed with watching and with tears?
No marvel, then, though I mistake my view;
The sun itself sees not till heaven clears.
   O cunning love, with tears thou keep'st me blind,
   Lest eyes well-seeing thy foul faults should find.

NOTES: Recalling earlier poems acknowledging his mistress' departure from conventional notions of beauty, the poet here comments upon the power of Love (or Cupid) to blur the vision of those in love. **Line 1,** *what eyes*: what kind of eyes? **Line 4,** *censures*: judges; *falsely*: incorrectly, or dishonestly. **Line 5,** *false*: deceitful. **Line 6,** *What means*: how comes, or by what right causes. **Line 7,** *eye*: the poet is employing a pun on the word "aye." **Line 10,** *watching*: wakefulness. **Line 11,** *No marvel*: it is not surprising; *though I mistake my view*: that I do not see clearly. **Line 12,** *till heaven clears*: until the sky is cloudless. **Line 13,** *love*: in addition to the emotion, and Cupid, the poet is now invoking the mistress as well. **Line 14,** *foul faults*: physical defects, or moral failings.

149

Canst thou, O cruel! say I love thee not
When I against myself with thee partake?
Do I not think on thee, when I forgot
Am of myself, all tyrant, for thy sake?
Who hateth thee that I do call my friend?
On whom frown'st thou that I do fawn upon?
Nay, if thou lour'st on me, do I not spend
Revenge upon myself with present moan?
What merit do I in myself respect
That is so proud thy service to despise,
When all my best doth worship thy defect,
Commanded by the motion of thine eyes?
   But, love, hate on, for now I know thy mind;
   Those that can see thou lovest, and I am blind.

NOTES: The poet now insists that he proves his love by taking the subject's side against all others—including the poet himself. **Line 2,** *I against myself with thee partake*: I side with you against myself (or, even against my better judgment). **Line 3,** *on*: about. **Lines 3-4,** *forgot am of myself*: when I forget about, or neglect, myself. **Line 4,** *all tyrant*: you utter tyrant. **Line 7:** *lour'st*: lower yourself (the sexual pun is intentional, especially in light of the lines that follow), or scowl at; *spend*: take. **Line 8,** *present moan*: immediate suffering. **Line 11:** *thy defect*: your lack of beauty. **Line 14,** *blind*: ie, unable to see your defects.

150

O, from what power hast thou this powerful might
With insufficiency my heart to sway,
To make me give the lie to my true sight,
And swear that brightness doth not grace the day?
Whence hast thou this becoming of things ill,
That in the very refuse of thy deeds
There is such strength and warrantise of skill
That, in my mind, thy worst all best exceeds?
Who taught thee how to make me love thee more,
The more I hear and see just cause of hate?
O, though I love what others do abhor,
With others thou shouldst not abhor my state.
  If thy unworthiness raised love in me,
  More worthy I to be beloved of thee.

NOTES: The poet concludes that loving his mistress despite her obvious faults makes him worthier of her love in return. **Line 2,** *With insufficiency*: despite all your defects. **Line 3,** *give the lie to my true sight*: accuse my eyes of lying to me about what I see. **Line 5,** *Whence hast thou this becoming of things ill*: where do you get the power to make evil so attractive. **Line 7,** *warrantise*: assurance or guarantee. **Line 12,** *With others*: like or along with other people (or lying with other men). **Line 14,** *More worthy I*: I am more entitled or deserving.

151

Love is too young to know what conscience is,
Yet who knows not conscience is born of love?
Then, gentle cheater, urge not my amiss,
Lest guilty of my faults thy sweet self prove.
For, thou betraying me, I do betray
My nobler part to my gross body's treason.
My soul doth tell my body that he may
Triumph in love; flesh stays no farther reason,
But, rising at thy name, doth point out thee
As his triumphant prize. Proud of this pride,
He is contented thy poor drudge to be,
To stand in thy affairs, fall by thy side.
   No want of conscience hold it that I call
   Her "love" for whose dear love I rise and fall.

NOTES: In a bawdy poem charged with thinly veiled sensuality, the poet ponders the power of sexual attraction over reason. **Line 1,** *Love*: ie, Cupid, often portrayed as a young boy. **Line 3,** *gentle cheater*: dear deceiver (spoken to the mistress); *urge not my amiss*: do not encourage my own misbehavior (or, do not emphasize my failings). **Line 5,** *betraying*: seducing. **Line 6,** *gross*: unrefined, or sensual. **Line 8,** *stays no farther reason*: abides no further argument, or needs no futher encouragement. **Lines 9-14:** the sexual imagery is intentional. **Line 10,** *Proud of this pride*: ie, swelling with, among other things, pride. **Line 13,** *want*: lack, or deficiency.

152

In loving thee thou know'st I am forsworn,
But thou art twice forsworn, to me love swearing;
In act thy bed-vow broke, and new faith torn
In vowing new hate after new love bearing.
But why of two oaths' breach do I accuse thee
When I break twenty? I am perjured most,
For all my vows are oaths but to misuse thee,
And all my honest faith in thee is lost.
For I have sworn deep oaths of thy deep kindness,
Oaths of thy love, thy truth, thy constancy,
And to enlighten thee gave eyes to blindness,
Or made them swear against the thing they see.
   For I have sworn thee fair; more perjured eye,
   To swear against the truth so foul a lie!

NOTES: Here, the poet acknowledges that his mistress is no more inconstant than he is. (Shakespeare was not only a married man, but also a friend to one of his mistress' lovers). **Line 1,** *I am forsworn*: I break my vow to another. **Line 3,** *In act*: ie, through sexual relations; *bed-vow*: marriage vow; *new faith torn*: a new oath broken. **Line 4,** *vowing*: promising; *new love bearing*: receiving the affections of someone new. **Line 5,** *breach*: violation. **Line 6,** *perjured most*: more guilty (of violating oaths). **Line 7,** *misuse*: deceive, or use for purposes of debauchery. **Line 8,** *honest faith*: trust; *in thee is lost*: ie, my faith in you has vanished (or, my debaucher's oath to misuse you vanishes inside you). **Line 9,** *deep*: heartfelt (the sexual play on words is probably intentional). **Line 11,** *enlighten*: to make you seem beautiful; *gave eyes to blindness*: turned a blind eye to the truth. **Line 13,** *eye*: a pun, invoking the homonyms "aye" and "I."

153

Cupid laid by his brand, and fell asleep.
A maid of Dian's this advantage found,
And his love-kindling fire did quickly steep
In a cold valley-fountain of that ground,
Which borrowed from this holy fire of Love
A dateless lively heat, still to endure,
And grew a seething bath, which yet men prove
Against strange maladies a sovereign cure.
But at my mistress' eye Love's brand new-fired,
The boy for trial needs would touch my breast;
I, sick withal, the help of bath desired,
And thither hied, a sad distempered guest,
    But found no cure. The bath for my help lies
    Where Cupid got new fire—my mistress' eyes.

NOTES: The next two poems recount an old parable, dating from Greek mythology. It is possible that one of them is an early draft of the other. **Line 1,** *laid by*: put aside; *brand*: fire or torch. **Line 2,** *Dian*: Diana, the Roman's goddess of the hunt, as well as chastity. She was served by a host of virgin nymphs. **Line 4,** *of that ground*: nearby. **Line 6,** *dateless*: eternal; *still*: forever. **Line 7,** *seething bath*: a hot spring. The reference may be to the natural hot springs at Bath, which were thought to have healing or curative powers. **Line 9,** *Love*: ie, Cupid; *new-fired*: became reignited. **Line 10,** *for trial*: for a test. **Line 11,** *sick withal*: sick as a result (of Cupid's torch). **Line 12,** *hied*: hurried; *distempered*: diseased.

154

The little Love-god, lying once asleep,
Laid by his side his heart-inflaming brand,
Whilst many nymphs that vowed chaste life to keep
Came tripping by; but in her maiden hand
The fairest votary took up that fire
Which many legions of true hearts had warmed,
And so the general of hot desire
Was, sleeping, by a virgin hand disarmed.
This brand she quenchèd in a cool well by,
Which from Love's fire took heat perpetual,
Growing a bath and healthful remedy
For men diseased; but I, my mistress' thrall,
   Came there for cure, and this by that I prove:
   Love's fire heats water, water cools not love.

NOTES: This last sonnet takes us down the same pathway through the woods as the previous one. **Line 1,** *Love-god*: Cupid. **Line 2,** *brand*: torch. **Line 5,** *fairest votary*: prettiest virgin. **Line 7,** *general of hot desire*: ie, Cupid. **Line 8,** *was sleeping by a virgin hand disarmed*: was, while asleep, disarmed by a virgin. **Line 11,** *Growing*: becoming.

REFERENCES AND RESOURCES

Bibliography and Suggested Reading

Ashton, Geoffrey. *Shakespeare: His Life and Works in Paintings, Prints and Ephemera.* London: Studio Editions, 1990.

Bloom, Harold. *Shakespeare: The Invention of the Human.* New York: Riverhead Books, 1998.

Booth, Stephen, ed. *Shakespeare's Sonnets.* New Haven: Yale University Press, 1977.

Chesterton, G. K., and Dorothy E. Collins. *Chesterton on Shakespeare.* London: Darwen Finlayson, 1971.

Crystal, David and Ben Crystal. *Shakespeare's Words: A Glossary and Language Companion.* New York: Penguin Books, 2002.

Duncan-Jones, Katherine, ed. *Shakespeare's Sonnets (Arden Shakespeare Edition).* London: Arden, 1997.

Eccles, Mark, *Shakespeare in Warwickshire.* Madison: University of Wisconsin Press, 1961.

Evans, G. Blakemore, ed. *The Sonnets (The New Cambridge Shakespeare).* Cambridge: Cambridge University Press, 1996.

Greenblatt, Stephen, ed. *The Norton Shakespeare.* New York: WW Norton, 1997.

_____. *Will in the World: How Shakespeare Became Shakespeare.* New York: WW Norton, 2004.

Grose, Francis. *The Vulgar Tongue.* Sussex: Summersdale, 2004.

Harrison, G.B. *Elizabethan Plays and Players*. Ann Arbor: University of Michigan Press, 1956.

Harrison, G.B, ed. *Shakespeare: The Complete Works*. New York: Hartcourt, Brace, 1968.

Herrnstein, Barbara, ed. *Discussions of Shakespeare's Sonnets*. Boston: DC Heath, 1964).

Ingram, W.G. and Theodore Redpath, eds. *Shakespeare's Sonnets*. London: University of London Press, 1967).

Kay, Dennis. *Shakespeare: His Life, Work, and Era*. New York: Wm. Morrow, 1992.

Kernan, Alvin B., ed. *Modern Shakespearean Criticism: Essays on Style, Dramaturgy, and the Major Plays*. New York, Hartcourt Brace, 1970.

Kiernan, Pauline. *Filthy Shakespeare: Shakespeare's Most Outrageous Sexual Puns*. New York: Gotham, 2007.

Kerrigan, John, ed. *The Sonnets and A Lover's Complaint (The New Penguin Shakespeare Edition)*. New York: New Penguin, 1986.

Lever, J.W. *The Elizabethan Love Sonnet (2d Ed)*. London: Methuen, 1966).

Levi, Peter. *The Life and Times of William Shakespeare*. New York: Henry Holt, 1988.

McGinn, Colin. *Shakespeare's Philosophy: Discovering the Meaning Behind the Plays*. New York, HarperCollins, 2006.

Mowat, Barbara and Paul Werstine, ed. *Shakespear's Sonnet (Folger Library Edition)*. New York: Washington Square Press, 2004.

Orgel, Stephen, ed. *The Sonnets (The Pelican Shakespeare Edition)*. New York: Pelican, 2001.

Schiffer, James, ed. *Shakespeare's Sonnets: Critical Essays*. New York: Garland, 1999.

Schoenbaum, Samuel. *William Shakespeare: A Documentary Life*. Oxford: Oxford University Press, 1975.

Vendler, Helen, ed. *The Art of Shakespeare's Sonnets*. Cambridge: Belknap Press, 1997.

Willen, Gerald, and Victor B. Reed, eds. *A Casebook on Shakespeare's Sonnets*. New York: Crowell, 1964.

Wrightson, Keith. *English Society, 1580-1680*. New Brunswick: Rutgers University Press, 1985.

Index to Commentary

Index to Commentary

Index to Commentary

Index of First Lines

(by Sonnet Number)

Index of First Lines

Index of First Lines

Index of First Lines

ABOUT THE AUTHOR

Born in 1564 in Stratford-upon-Avon, William Shakespeare moved to London in the late 1580s to seek his fame and fortune, leaving his wife and children behind in Stratford. He soon became a well-known actor and theater owner, and began writing plays for his acting company. His first play opened in 1592 to rave reviews, and he turned his attention to poetry and playwriting, as well as acting. Widely acclaimed during his lifetime, his best-loved works include tragedies such as *Hamlet* and *Macbeth*; comedies, such as *Twelfth Night* and *The Tempest*; and historical dramas depicting the perils and triumphs of English royalty. His sonnets, a collection of poems written over a long period of time, were privately circulated among patrons and friends throughout his career until their initial publication in 1609. Having made his fortune largely in the entertainment industry, Shakespeare retired in 1610, returning to Stratford after a career spanning two decades and more than three dozen plays. He died in 1616.